30 Ten-Minute Plays for 2 Actors
from Actors Theatre of Louisville's National Ten-Minute Play Contest

30 Ten-Minute Plays for 2 Actors
from Actors Theatre of Louisville's National Ten-Minute Play Contest

Edited by Michael Bigelow Dixon,
Amy Wegener, and Karen C. Petruska

Contemporary Playwrights Series

SK
A Smith and Kraus Book

A Smith and Kraus Book
Published by Smith and Kraus, Inc.
177 Lyme Road, Hanover, NH 03755
www.SmithandKraus.com

Manufactured in the United States of America

Cover and Text Design by Julia Hill Gignoux, Freedom Hill Design
Layout by Jennifer McMaster
Cover Photograph by Richard Trigg
Cover Photograph: *Drive Angry* by Matt Pelfrey
(l-r: Bryan Richards, Derek Cecil)

First Edition: September 2001
8 7 6 5 4 3 2 1

Library of Congress Cataloging-in-Publication Data
30 ten-minute plays for 2 actors, from The National Ten-Minute Play Contest / edited by Michael Bigelow Dixon, Amy Wegener, and Karen C. Petruska. —1st ed.
p. cm. — (Contemporary playwrights series)
ISBN 1-57525-277-5 (v.1)
ISBN 978-1-57525-277-3
1. One-act plays, American. 2. American drama—20th century. I. Title: Thirty ten-minute plays for 2 actors, from the National Ten-Minute Play Contest. II. Dixon, Michael Bigelow. III. Wegener, Amy. IV. Petruska, Karen C. V. Series.

PS627.O53 A16 2001
812'.04108054—dc21   2001032198

Contents

Acknowledgments

Thanks to the following persons for their invaluable assistance in compiling this volume of plays:

Brendan Healy

Jennifer McMaster

Stephen Moulds

Emily Roderer

Jeffrey Rodgers

Jimmy Seacat

Alexander Speer

Richard Trigg

Introduction

Here it is—the first of three volumes which together feature ninety of the best ten-minute plays written by American playwrights at the turn of the 21st century. Thanks to Smith and Kraus, these plays are published in a usable format for actors and directors, teachers, and students. Organized by cast size and character gender, each of these three collections of thirty plays offers plenty of choice in subject matter and style. And though the form is compact by definition, each play offers ample opportunity for actors to stretch themselves by delving into the dynamics of conflict between two characters. Accusation, negotiation, confrontation, intimidation, accommodation, and consolation—these actions and others make this volume a veritable casebook in human psychology.

Over the past two decades, the ten-minute play has established itself as a potent and durable form in American theater. One reason is that these are complete plays—with beginnings, middles, and ends; scenic and sound requirements; images and ideas; and arguments engaged and resolved. As such, they make the same demands and require the same creative work as longer plays but within a more manageable package.

Another reason for the form's popularity is that its brevity relates directly to the restlessness of the American character. Americans aren't about lingering or loitering—my God, we even have laws against it!—and neither are these plays. Things *happen* in these plays! Because they move so quickly, the plays are just long enough to satisfy the American need to get to the root of problems and short enough to allow us to move along once the dramatic problem's been dealt with.

Truth to tell, however, this is a collection of work over which you might wish to linger, to savor the ingenuity and insight of authors who know whereof they write. Sure, the ten-minute play is American culture writ small, but so is the soundbite, the headline, the commercial, the cartoon, the news feature, the magazine story, the billboard, the photograph, and the editorial. Each of these short forms has its role in our culture, each reveals a facet of who we are and how we work, and each is here to stay. Brevity in perpetuity.

Michael Bigelow Dixon, Amy Wegener, Karen C. Petruska

Plays
for
Two Women

Misreadings
by Neena Beber

1

CHARACTERS

SIMONE
RUTH

Misreadings

Lights up on Simone.

SIMONE: It's important to dress right. I want to look slick. To look sleek. To look like a fresh thing. I've got a message. I'm the message. Study me, baby, because in ten minutes, I'm outta here.
(Simone lights a cigarette. Lights up on Ruth.)

RUTH: What are the issues for which you would kill? I like to ask my students this on their first day of class. I assign novels where the hero or heroine kills or is killed. I try to bring it home. They tell me they would kill to defend their family. They'd kill to defend their friends. I ask them if they would kill for their country...for their freedom...what would it take?

SIMONE: I'd kill for a pair of Prada velvet platforms in deep plum. *Those* are to die for.

RUTH: Simone. I didn't know what she was doing in my class. Neither did she, apparently. *(To Simone.)* Nice segue, Simone; would we be willing to die for the same things we'd kill for? *(Out.)* I wanted her to participate. She usually sat in the back, never spoke, wore too much lipstick and some costume straight out of, what, *Vogue.* When she did speak, it was always—disruptive.

SIMONE: I'd die for love except there ain't no Romeos, not that I've seen; I'd take a bullet for my daddy but he's already dead; I'd die of boredom if it were lethal, but I guess it isn't.

RUTH: If I couldn't inspire her, I wanted her gone. I'd asked her to come to my office hours. I asked her several times. She was failing, obviously. I would have let her drop the class, but it was too late for that. She never bothered to come see me. Not until the day before the final exam. She wanted me to give her a passing grade. *(Ruth turns to Simone.)* How can I do that, Simone? You haven't even read the material. Have you read *any* of the material?

SIMONE: I don't find it relevant.

RUTH: If you haven't read it, how do you know? You may find yourself surprised. *Anna Karenina* is wonderful.

SIMONE: It's long.

RUTH: Why not give it a shot?

SIMONE: The books you assign are depressing. I don't want to be depressed. Why read stuff that brings you down? Kafka, Jesus Christ—I started it, OK? The guy was fucked up.

RUTH: So you were moved at least.

SIMONE: Moved to shut the book and find something more interesting to do.

RUTH: That's too bad; you might find one of these books getting under your skin if you stick with it. Haven't you ever read something that's really moved you?

SIMONE: Nothing moves me, Dr. Ruth.

RUTH: I'm going to have to ask you to put out that cigarette.

SIMONE: OK, ask. *(She puts it out.)* See art or be art. I choose the latter.

RUTH: Somebody must be paying for this education of yours. I imagine they expect a certain return for their money.

SIMONE: How do you know I'm not the one paying for it?

RUTH: I don't believe someone who was spending their own money would waste it so flagrantly.

SIMONE: Okay, Dad chips in.

RUTH: Would that be the same father you said was dead?

SIMONE: That was a joke or a lie, take your pick.

RUTH: You're frustrating the hell out of me, Simone.

SIMONE: I don't consider it a waste, you know. I like the socialization part.

RUTH: If you fail out of this school, you won't be doing any more "social-ization."

SIMONE: You assume that I'm failing the others.

RUTH: So it's just this class, then? That you have a problem with?

SIMONE: Dangling. *(Referring to her grammar.)* Do you enjoy being a teacher?

RUTH: Yes, I do.

SIMONE: So I'm paying for your enjoyment.

RUTH: It's not a sin to enjoy one's work, Simone.

SIMONE: I just don't think you should charge me if it's more for your pleasure than for mine.

RUTH: I didn't say that.

SIMONE: Did you ever want to teach at a real school, not some second-rate institution like this?

RUTH: I like my job. You're not going to convince me otherwise.

SIMONE: Four thousand two hundred and ninety-eight.

RUTH: That is—?

SIMONE: Dollars. That's a lot of money. Do you think you're worth it? Do you think *this class* is worth it? Because I figured it out: this is a four-credit class, I broke it down. Four thousand two hundred and ninety-eight. Big ones. Well, do you think that what you have to teach me is worth that? Come on, start talking and we'll amortize for each word.

RUTH: You're clearly a bright girl. You can't expect an education to be broken down into monetary terms.

SIMONE: You just did. That's a lot of money, right? It's, like, food for a starving family in a fifth-world country for a year at least. It's a car. Well, a used one, anyway. Minus the insurance. Suddenly this number doesn't sound so huge. It's a couple of Armani suits at most. I don't even like Armani. So hey, come on, can't you even say, "Yes, Simone, I am worth two Armani suits. I have that to offer you…"

RUTH: I can't say that, no.

SIMONE: No useful skills to be had here.

RUTH: The money doesn't go into my pocket, by the way.

SIMONE: I think it should. It would be more direct that way; you'd feel more of a responsibility. To me. Personally. Don't you think, Dr. Ruth?

RUTH: I'd prefer that you not call me that.

SIMONE: But your name is Ruth, and…you do have a Ph.D., don't you?

RUTH: OK, Simone.

SIMONE: Wrong kind of doctor, man. All you're interested in is a bunch of books written a hundred years ago, and the books written about those books; you're probably writing a book about a book written about a book right now, am I right?

RUTH: If you don't see the connection of books to life, you aren't reading very well. I want you to try. Can you do that? Books might even show you a way to live.

SIMONE: I'm already living, Dr. Ruth. Are you? Because it looks like you haven't changed your hair style in twenty-five years.

RUTH: *(Insulted but covering.)* Well, that's before you were born, Simone.

SIMONE: Stuck in your best year? Because I see you in a close-cropped, spiky thing.

RUTH: That's enough. We're here to think, Simone, you are correct in that. We read these books and talk about what we've read with a certain discipline so that we might sharpen our minds, our sensitivity.

SIMONE: It's not going to get me anywhere. A sensitive mind. I don't need that. I can't use that. So what you're offering me, I don't need it. I don't even like the way you dress.

RUTH: Have you been in therapy?

SIMONE: Don't think that's an original suggestion.

RUTH: I'm not suggesting anything. I simply want to point out that this is not therapy. I am a teacher, not your therapist. You can't just waltz into my office and say whatever hateful thing you please.

SIMONE: I don't know how to waltz.

RUTH: I'm giving up here, Simone. You don't like my class, you don't like me, you want to fail out, I can't stop you. *(Ruth goes back to her work. Simone does not budge. Ruth finally looks up.)* What?

SIMONE: Drew Barrymore would move me.

RUTH: Who?

SIMONE: I think Drew would do it. Getting to meet Drew.

RUTH: Who's Drew Barrymore?

SIMONE: Damn, you really should know these things. She's extremely famous. She's been famous since she was, like, born. I saw her on TV yesterday and she was so real. She connected. You know? You really might relate to your students better if you got a little more up-to-date.

RUTH: You might be right. But you might not be so behind in class if you spent a little less time watching television.

SIMONE: Drew is a *film* star, she's in *films*. Don't you even go to the movies? Probably only the ones that are totally L-Seven. And I know you don't know what that means. *(She makes an 'L' and a '7' with her fingers.)* Square? Anyway, Drew was on TV because she was being interviewed. They have these daytime talk shows nowadays?

RUTH: I've heard of them.

SIMONE: And this chick was in the audience and she started to cry. Because she couldn't believe she was there in the same room with Drew, who's been famous forever, right? She was just, like, sitting there sobbing. And this chick, she had her bleached blond hair pasted down real flat, and she was wearing a rhinestone barrette just like Drew used to, but that whole look is so old Drew, so ten-minutes-ago Drew. The new Drew is sleek and sophisticated and coiffed and this girl, this girl who wanted to be Drew so bad, she wasn't even *current*.

RUTH: I don't think we're getting anywhere.

SIMONE: And that is so sad. Because the thing about Drew is, she is always changing. It's a constant thing with her, the change. And that is, like, what you've got to do…keep moving or you die. Drew knows that. How to invent yourself again and again so you can keep being someone that you like, the someone that you want to be. And once you're it, you've got to move on. Now where was it you were hoping we'd get to?

RUTH: The exam is tomorrow morning at 9 AM. If you read the material, any of the material, I might actually be able to give you a passing grade. But right now I don't think we need to waste any more of each other's time.

SIMONE: *(Starts to go.)* You might have said that I go to the movies the way you read books. I would have pointed that out, Dr. Ruth.

RUTH: Yes. Well. I suspect we don't think very much alike.

SIMONE: A wall between our souls? *(Ruth looks at her, about to say something, about to reach out.)* I'm sorry if I've been rude. I'm sure a lot of people like your class. Maybe I wasn't raised well. I'm sure somebody's to blame. *(Simone goes to write in a blue exam book.)*

RUTH: The next day she showed up at nine on the dot. I felt a certain pride that I had somehow managed to reach her, that she was finally going to make a real effort, but she handed in her blue book after a matter of minutes. I was rather disgusted and let it sit there, until a pile formed on top of it, a pile of blue books filled with the scrawling, down-to-the-last-second pages of my other more eager, or at least more dutiful, students. Later I began to read them straight through from the top, in the order they were stacked in. I wasn't looking forward to Simone's.

In answering my essay question about how the novel *Anna Karenina* moves inevitably toward Anna's final tragic act, my students were, for the most part, thorough and precise. They cited the events that led to Anna's throwing herself in front of the train, touching on the parallel plots and the broader social context. I was satisfied. I felt I had taught well this last semester. My students had learned.

In the blue book she had written, "All happy people resemble one another, but each unhappy person is unhappy in their own way." So I guess she had read Anna K; the opening sentence, at least. My first instinct was to correct the grammar of her little variation. There was nothing else on the page. I flipped through the book; she'd written one more line on the last page: "Any world that I'm welcome to is better than the one that I come from." I'm told it's a rock lyric. Something from the seventies. *Anna* was written in the seventies, too, funnily enough, a century earlier.

I would have given Simone an F, but I noticed she had already marked down the failing grade herself, on the back of the book. Or maybe the grade was for me.

By the time I came to it, days had passed. I didn't leap to conclusions. Come to think of it, Anna's suicide always takes me by surprise as well, though I've read the novel many times and can map its inexorable progression.

(Simone, just as before…)

SIMONE: That's a lot of money. Do you think you're worth it? Do you think this class is worth it? *(Ruth turns to her, wanting to reach out.)*

RUTH: I live in worlds made by words. Worlds where the dead can speak, and conversations can be replayed, altered past the moment of regret, held over and over until they are bent into new possibilities.

SIMONE: Do you think I'm worth it? Am I? Am I? Am I?

RUTH: I live there, where death is as impermanent as an anesthesia, and the moment of obliteration is only…a blackout.

(Simone lights a cigarette as lights black out.)

SIMONE: Ten minutes, time's up—told you I'd be gone by now, baby.

(The flame illuminates her for a moment, darkness again.)

END OF PLAY

Happy Mug
by Elizabeth Dewberry

CHARACTERS
CAROLE

ANNA

Happy Mug

Carole and Anna, sisters, in their early twenties, are in the flower shop where they work. Carole is working on the books, punching numbers into an adding machine. Anna is making a little flower arrangement in a coffee cup for a new mother—carnations and baby's breath.

ANNA: Joe said Heather was in labor for thirty-eight hours, and then they did a C-section.

CAROLE: I know. After all that, he should have sprung for a better arrangement.

ANNA: I think the thrill is gone. Remember when he used to come in every Friday afternoon and get her a red rose?

CAROLE: From that to Happy Mugs. The next step is, no flowers at all. Or, worse, nothing but a white orchid on Mother's Day.

ANNA: What's wrong with orchids?

CAROLE: They have *nothing* to do with sex. And the men who give them to the mothers of their children are so worn out that they haven't even noticed. *(Beat. Anna consciously changes the subject.)*

ANNA: I'm going to stop by McDonald's on the way back from delivering this. You want anything?

CAROLE: Not from McDonald's.

ANNA: I'm in the mood for a fish sandwich. McFish.

CAROLE: It's not McFish. It's Filet-O-Fish.

ANNA: With lots of catsup. I'm going to get me two of them.

CAROLE: I couldn't get enough of those when I was pregnant, but now I can't stand them. I've vomited up too many of them. Have you ever vomited catsup?

ANNA: No.

CAROLE: I thought it was blood.

ANNA: Well, thank you for sharing.

CAROLE: Damn. I can't get these numbers to add up to the same thing twice. *(She stops adding to pour herself a cup of coffee.)*

ANNA: You okay?

CAROLE: I'm just tired. The baby had me up all night, screaming.

ANNA: You screamed at her all night?

CAROLE: Ha ha. I swear I felt like it, though.

ANNA: I didn't sleep much last night, either, but I *was* screaming.

CAROLE: Uh-oh.

ANNA: Not screaming. Just...dis*cus*sing.

CAROLE: Right. What are you doing Saturday night?

ANNA: What I always do on Saturday nights—nothing. Brad's watching a pay-per-view fight. He told me to get him two six-packs and a frozen pizza. I said, why do you have to pay forty dollars to watch a fight when I'll argue with you for free?

CAROLE: Want to babysit?

ANNA: No.

CAROLE: Spend a little quality time with your niece?

ANNA: *No.*

CAROLE: What's the difference? You already bring Brad a bottle every hour or so. And you already put up with his shit.

ANNA: I don't put up with shit.

CAROLE: Come on. I really need a night to myself. I haven't had any fun since Zelda was born. The only dinners out I've eaten have been Happy Meals, I haven't seen a movie, I haven't had a conversation that didn't include the word cholic—

ANNA: Ask Mom.

CAROLE: She can't until her ear gets better.

ANNA: What's wrong with her ear?

CAROLE: My guess is, it's tired of hearing Zelda scream.

ANNA: Ask Dad and Stephanie.

CAROLE: They won't do it on weekends. Conveniently, since I'm too exhausted to go out during the week.

ANNA: Randy's still the great invisible dad? *(Carole answers with silence: Anna already knows the answer to that question. Anna gets out a cigarette, again trying to change the subject, but doesn't light it. Carole looks at it disapprovingly.)* I'm trying to quit. I've got the patch, but it's not helping. *(She shows it to Carole by pulling up her sleeve.)* I should paint it black and wear it over my eye. *(Carole's still upset.)* Get two of them, put glitter on them and wear them as pasties. Think Brad would look up from the fight for that? *(No response. Anna gives up. They're back to a tense silence.)*

CAROLE: I'm not asking for a village here. I'm asking for a couple of hours a week of help, while I handle the other six days and twenty-two hours for the next eighteen years by myself. *(Anna shows some irritation.)* Seriously, what man is going to—

ANNA: *(Softly.)* Shut up.

CAROLE: You have no idea how hard it is to spend your entire night, night after night, with a person who can't walk, can't feed herself, can't have a conversation, can't do anything but shit, vomit, and scream. And I look at my friends who have two- and three-year-olds, and it changes, but it doesn't get any better. Have you ever spent an entire day alone with a three-year-old?

ANNA: No.

CAROLE: Even if it's a good kid, it's just so boring. I babysat Ann Marie while Heather was in labor—

ANNA: She's cute.

CAROLE: She's adorable and smart and articulate for a three-year-old, but by two o'clock, I was so lonely I was about to cry. I mean, how long can you sustain an interest in Scooby-Doo? How many times can you tuck a teddy bear into bed—we tucked stuffed animals into every bed, real or imaginary, in the house. If she weren't three, she'd be crazy. I felt like I *was* crazy. Please, just give me a break.

ANNA: Please shut up. *(She starts to light her cigarette.)*

CAROLE: Stop it. I don't want your second-hand smoke.

ANNA: *(Stubbing out the cigarette.)* And I don't want your second-hand baby. *(Carole is visibly stunned and hurt.)* I'm sorry. I didn't mean...I'm sorry.

CAROLE: You can't even bring yourself to say you didn't mean it because you did.

ANNA: No, I didn't.

CAROLE: Nobody who doesn't have a baby can possibly understand. I mean, you're not supposed to talk about it or you're a bad mother—you might mention postpartum blues and then everybody just says how wonderful having a baby is. It's a conspiracy of silence. But I'm telling you, and you know I love Zelda, I would give up anything for her, but sometimes I just feel like I cannot look at another dirty diaper, I can't go another night without sleep, I can't wipe the vomit out of my hair with a napkin on my way out the door, I can't—

ANNA: Would you *shut up?*

CAROLE: What is your problem? *(Tense pause.)*

ANNA: *(Quietly.)* I'm pregnant. *(Beat.)*

CAROLE: Really? *(Anna lets out a one-syllable laugh/sigh and shakes her head. Beat.)* Well, Anna, that's…wonderful.

ANNA: Please.

CAROLE: Oh, I'm so happy for you. Congratulations.

ANNA: I was on birth control. I don't know what happened.

CAROLE: We can babysit for each other! And you can have all my hand-me-downs, and Zelda will be out of her crib by then, so you can—

ANNA: I don't know if I'm going to keep it. *(Beat.)*

CAROLE: Of course you will. You'll fall in love at first sight. The second they put her in your arms, you'll forget all the pain, and you won't be able to think of giving her away. Or him.

ANNA: I'm not talking about adoption. *(Pause.)*

CAROLE: Anna, I was *venting*. I thought you were the one person I could do that with. But I didn't mean it the way it sounded.

ANNA: It sounded pretty clear.

CAROLE: Don't you ever say anything you don't mean? Or out of context?

ANNA: Name a context where what you just said—

CAROLE: Or you exaggerate because you want—

ANNA: No, I don't.

CAROLE: Everybody does. You can't do this.

ANNA: You know what you can and can't do—you can't look at another diaper, but you *have* to—and I know what *I* can and can't do, and *I* don't have to.

CAROLE: But, I mean, you don't know… Just this morning, I walk into Zelda's room—she's crying—and I start singing to her—I haven't even picked her up yet, and she stops just because she hears my voice. I mean that's…it's primal. All the other stuff disappears in the face of that. I can't explain.

ANNA: Yeah, everybody says having a baby is wonderful. But everybody says things they don't mean. *(Beat.)*

CAROLE: You know what I craved when I was pregnant? McDonald's fish sandwiches.

ANNA: You told me that.

CAROLE: And I haven't had one since, but let's go get some.

ANNA: No.

CAROLE: We'll close the shop for an hour. Nobody'll know. Suddenly I'm feeling deprived of McFish.

ANNA: Filet-O-Fish.

CAROLE: I think they're better than the Cajun Cupboard's, except they're not Cajun, but they're just as good, and they're, like, two dollars, where Cajun Cupboard's are, what, seven? Eight dollars?

ANNA: Four ninety-five.

CAROLE: You can get two McDonald's for less than that. Come on, I'm gonna take you to McDonald's and get us some Filet-O-Fish sandwiches with pickles on them—

ANNA: I hate pickles.

CAROLE: Have it your way. And those little packets of catsup—they're better than catsup out of a bottle, I don't know why, but don't you think?—and some fries. I love McDonald's fries. You want a milkshake, too? Lots of calcium.

ANNA: I thought you were sick of McDonald's.

CAROLE: No, I'm...I *love* McDonald's. Okay, I have my moments, but Anna, McDonald's is part of life. I mean seriously, Lord help me the day when I decide to cut out Happy Meals forever just because I'm tired one day, or bored or grumpy. I mean, it's one thing to let off steam, but that's like...cutting out a part of myself.

ANNA: *(Referring to a part of Carole where some fat is.)* This part?

CAROLE: *(Very seriously.)* It is. I couldn't do it. And if *I'm* sometimes a little tired of...McDonald's, it doesn't automatically translate that you would be. You might *love* those fish sandwiches. I bet you would. *I* know you would. Because I do too. Please, Anna.

ANNA: That doesn't automatically translate either. *(Beat.)*

CAROLE: You don't want to spend the rest of your life wondering what would have been, do you?

ANNA: No, but I also want to *have* a life.

CAROLE: You have a life.

ANNA: You just explained to me in great detail how you have no life.

CAROLE: I *told* you, I was—

ANNA: *(Overlapping.)* I don't want to feel that way.

CAROLE: No, you'd rather sit in your kitchen doing crossword puzzles while Brad watches fights on T.V. Nobody'd blame you for not wanting to give up that. *(Beat.)*

ANNA: Are you happy?

CAROLE: What?

ANNA: Are you happy? It's not that complicated a question.

CAROLE: Yes it is.

ANNA: Well are you?

CAROLE: I don't know. What's your point?

ANNA: My point is, what's the point?

CAROLE: Of what?

ANNA: I'm afraid. I'm afraid of being in labor for thirty-eight hours and then being cut open while I'm wide awake. I'm afraid something will be wrong with the baby and I won't know what to do about it. I'm afraid of being a bad mother and fucking up my kid without even realizing I'm doing it and the kid grows up to hate me. I'm afraid of Brad being a bad father and me growing to hate him for it. *And* I'm afraid of *not* risking all that just because I was too afraid…. I'm afraid I'll never be happy, and I'll get to a place where I don't even see the point of asking whether I am. *(Long pause.)* I'm sorry. *(Carole picks up the Happy Mug and hands it to Anna.)*

CAROLE: Here. Give Heather my love, okay? *(Beat.)*

ANNA: Yeah. *(Anna pauses, then turns to go.)*

CAROLE: And get me a happy meal? *(Beat.)*

ANNA: Sure.

(Anna exits. Carole pauses, then goes back to adding on the adding machine as the lights fade to black.)

END OF PLAY

Kat and Eliza
by Ann Marie Healy

CHARACTERS

KAT

ELIZA

Kat and Eliza

Kat and Eliza at Kat's house.

KAT: I'm so glad you called me this morning. It's been too long... You look a lot older.

ELIZA: You look a lot older too.

KAT: I'm only two years older than you.

ELIZA: But you look a lot older.

KAT: You do too. *(Pause.)*

ELIZA: I said to myself this morning, I should call. And then I actually listened to myself. Have you ever listened to yourself Kat? You'd be surprised at the things you hear.

KAT: If you don't listen to yourself, who's going to listen to you. That's the lesson I've learned in life.

ELIZA: But no one wants to hear your lesson. That's my point. *(Pause.)*

KAT: How is Charles?

ELIZA: Oh, good... He's not special. Right now. He'll be something special later in life. I'm investing in the future on this one.

KAT: I was wondering what you were doing.

ELIZA: What about Lloyd...

KAT: I think. Well... We're trying to start a family. Lloyd and I are.

ELIZA: Sometimes I think about having a family too.

KAT: But Eliza! You have me. I'll always be your family.

ELIZA: Of course. But, maybe, I'd like to have my own family.

KAT: Me too. It would be so much better.

ELIZA: You would be good at having your own family. You were always good at owning things.

KAT: I like having things. I don't necessarily like owning them.

ELIZA: But babies. You would be better at owning your own babies.

KAT: Do you really think so?

ELIZA: I do. When babies sit on your lap they never want to leave. It's really cute.

KAT: That's what cinched it for me. I figured, if someone else's baby wants to be in my lap, imagine how much my own baby will want to be in my lap. That's when I knew I should be a mother.

ELIZA: Definitely… Except. Sometimes, when you actually own a baby, it doesn't want to be in your lap. I've noticed that with some babies.

KAT: That's what your baby would be like.

ELIZA: Yeah… Do you really think so?

KAT: It's not a bad thing.

ELIZA: Having a baby that wanted to run away from me?

KAT: An active baby. An early developer… I saw a baby yesterday with biceps. That's a good thing.

ELIZA: Mom told me that you were like that.

KAT: Really. I had biceps?

ELIZA: At a very young age… I thought you knew.

KAT: No. I never knew that about myself.

ELIZA: Mom and I used to talk about it all the time… Maybe I wasn't supposed to tell you that.

KAT: What else did Mom say?

ELIZA: You know Mom. She had lots of things to say. *(Pause.)*

KAT: I think she was relieved that you never talked about having children.

ELIZA: Did she say that?

KAT: I can't remember her exact words.

ELIZA: But she said she was relieved I never talked about having children.

KAT: That's what she said. *(Pause.)*

ELIZA: Kat… Do you think I would be a bad mother?

KAT: No. Not at all. I just don't think you should be a mother.

ELIZA: Charles said the exact same thing to me.

KAT: Eliza. You can't let him talk to you like that.

ELIZA: It's good to get those things out. We're not like you and Lloyd. We enjoy fighting.

KAT: Lloyd and I have great fights… Last night he threw spaghetti on the floor.

ELIZA: The actual pot or just the pasta?

KAT: Just the pasta. But it was uncooked so it made a noise. I'm sure the neighbors heard. How embarrassing.

ELIZA: I know it. Charles and I had it out last night too. He didn't throw anything, but he slammed a door in my face.

KAT: I told Lloyd last night that if he didn't start picking up his dirty laundry, he wasn't going to see morning.

ELIZA: I told Charles last night that I was pregnant.

KAT: What? *(Pause.)*

ELIZA: I'm going to have a baby.

KAT: I just told you I wanted to have a baby.

ELIZA: We can both have a baby.

KAT: I don't want to have a baby with you. *(Pause.)* Congratulations. *(Pause.)* Did you tell Mom?

ELIZA: You're the first to know.

KAT: Of course you told me first.

ELIZA: Did you tell Mom?

KAT: What?

ELIZA: About your baby?

KAT: I don't have a baby.

ELIZA: But you're going to.

KAT: I don't want to cry wolf.

ELIZA: That's not crying wolf. Saying you want something is not crying wolf. And Kat, you always get what you want.

KAT: I do, don't I? I want to so I will.

ELIZA: What's stopping you... *(Pause.)*

KAT: There are just some minor complications.

ELIZA: Oh no... With you.

KAT: No. Not me.

ELIZA: Lloyd?

KAT: Yes.

ELIZA: ...I think he's really a nice person.

KAT: He is. He's very sweet. *(Pause.)*

ELIZA: Thank you.

KAT: For what?

ELIZA: For telling me that.

KAT: You're welcome. *(Pause.)*

ELIZA: Maybe you can do something.

KAT: We're trying. I mean. We will do something. But it might take some time.

ELIZA: And. I'll be here for you.

KAT: Of course. I can call you if I want to talk to someone. Someone who is not Lloyd.

ELIZA: It's good to have someone to talk to when you want to talk about the person you usually talk to.

KAT: I have nothing bad to say about Lloyd. *(Pause.)* Where's my head. I could be there for you. And the baby.

ELIZA: Sure.

KAT: Let's talk about your baby right now.

ELIZA: I don't think that's a good idea.

KAT: Do you want a boy or a girl?

ELIZA: This will be painful for you.

KAT: Yes it will…but I don't mind.

ELIZA: And it's not a totally happy thing.

KAT: You're not totally happy with your thing?

ELIZA: Not really.

KAT: I see.

ELIZA: That's why Charles and I had the fight.

KAT: But you got everything out.

ELIZA: We always do. We know everything about each other.

KAT: Did you know he didn't want to have a baby?

ELIZA: I knew the moment he told me.

KAT: Eliza… Do you want to have a baby?

ELIZA: I don't know. What do you think?

KAT: How should I know what you think.

ELIZA: Not what I think. What you think. Do you think it's a good idea? *(Pause.)*

KAT: Poor Eliza.

ELIZA: Why did you just say "Poor Eliza."

KAT: Because this is so like you. Even after all these years, you still need me to tell you what to do.

ELIZA: You're good at it.

KAT: I always wondered what would happen to you when I wasn't there to wake you up in the morning. Do you act this way around Charles?

ELIZA: Kat. You're the only one who makes me act this way.

KAT: I don't make you do things. If I did, your life wouldn't be such a mess.

ELIZA: Do you really think my life is a mess?

KAT: Yes. I do… And I'm not trying to make you feel unhappy.

ELIZA: Then why do you always make me feel unhappy?

KAT: You make yourself feel unhappy.

ELIZA: I thought you were in charge.

KAT: The root of the problem is that you started listening to yourself.

ELIZA: The root of the problem is that you have always been jealous of me.

KAT: Eliza. I have never been jealous of you. *(Pause.)*

ELIZA: Well that's a relief isn't it. *(Pause.)* Not even a little jealous. Of Charles, for example?

KAT: No. *(Pause.)*

ELIZA: I don't know what to do with myself now.

KAT: What do you mean?

ELIZA: All my life. Everything I've ever done. It was always to get your attention.

KAT: I'm sorry it didn't work out, Eliza.

ELIZA: It's okay. I mean. I'm sure you tried.

KAT: I did try. I'm trying right now.

ELIZA: Do you even care that I'm having a baby?

KAT: I care that you are having a baby, Eliza.

ELIZA: Maybe I shouldn't have it.

KAT: No! *(Pause.)* Can I feel your stomach?

ELIZA: Of course you can. *(Pause.)* You know. After tonight, it's going to be okay. Everything between us. Finally. *(Kat places her hands on Eliza's stomach.)* Don't you feel that way?

KAT: Hmm…

(Kat puts her head on Eliza's stomach.)

ELIZA: I mean, don't you feel like everything is finally changing between us. *(Pause.)*

KAT: Yes. Yes I do, Eliza.

END OF PLAY

Nightswim
by Julia Jordan

CHARACTERS

ROSIE: Seventeen years old.
CHRISTINA: Seventeen years old.

Nightswim

Lights up outside Christina's house. It is midnight and her parents are asleep. Her bedroom window on the second floor is dark. Rosie is in the front yard.

ROSIE: *(Whispers loudly.)* Christina. Christina! *(Christina, dressed for bed in a ratty old T-shirt and underwear, comes to the window. She has not been sleeping.)*

CHRISTINA: What?

ROSIE: Come out and play.

CHRISTINA: We're too old to play.

ROSIE: Wanna do something?

CHRISTINA: What?

ROSIE: I don't know, something.

CHRISTINA: Like what?

ROSIE: Wanna go climb the railroad bridge? Cross the river?

CHRISTINA: We're too old to climb the railroad bridge.

ROSIE: Go skinny-dipping in the old man's pool?

CHRISTINA: He's always watching.

ROSIE: So?

CHRISTINA: It's undignified.

ROSIE: We'll go to the lake.

CHRISTINA: The police will catch us.

ROSIE: They haven't all summer.

CHRISTINA: We haven't gone all summer.

ROSIE: So they won't expect us.

CHRISTINA: It's cold.

ROSIE: That'll make the water feel warm, like swimming in velvet.

CHRISTINA: There's no lifeguard.

ROSIE: So we can swim naked.

CHRISTINA: What if we drown like the Berridges' boy? Our bodies would get caught under the weeping willow in the water. No one would find us for weeks.

ROSIE: We won't go anywhere near that tree.

CHRISTINA: But there's no lifeguard.

ROSIE: You forgot how to swim?

CHRISTINA: No.

ROSIE: Let's go.

CHRISTINA: I'm tired.

ROSIE: Skinny-dipping is like resting itself.

CHRISTINA: What if that rapist with the mustache and the beady eyes is out there?

ROSIE: He's in jail.

CHRISTINA: There could be another one. Beady-eyed rapists are a dime a dozen. A copycat crazy.

ROSIE: Black water, black night. He won't even see us.

CHRISTINA: Our skin glows like 60-watt bulbs at night.

ROSIE: The water will cover us.

CHRISTINA: He'll come in after us.

ROSIE: Rapists can't swim so good.

CHRISTINA: He'll get us on the beach.

ROSIE: You can run, can't you?

CHRISTINA: He has a fast car.

ROSIE: You can hide, can't you?

CHRISTINA: He carries a flashlight. He senses fear. He'll find me.

ROSIE: You can fight, can't you?

CHRISTINA: He's bigger than me.

ROSIE: You can scream, can't you?

CHRISTINA: No one will hear me.

ROSIE: I'll hear you. Two against one.

CHRISTINA: What if there are two of him? Or three? Or a gang of crazies hiding under the weeping willow tree waiting for us.

ROSIE: We won't go anywhere near that tree.

CHRISTINA: What if there are two?

ROSIE: What if there are none?

CHRISTINA: I can't.

ROSIE: You're scared?

CHRISTINA: Yes.

ROSIE: Admit it.

CHRISTINA: I do.

ROSIE: Say it.

CHRISTINA: I'm scared.

ROSIE: Don't be.

CHRISTINA: Why not?

ROSIE: 'Cause it's a beautiful night for a swim.

CHRISTINA: It is?

ROSIE: The water will be like swimming in black velvet because the air is cool. The lake will be all ours because everyone is locked up in sleep. We will swim naked because there is no lifeguard. And there won't be any crazies because I have a feeling. *(Beat.)* It's a beautiful night for a swim.

CHRISTINA: The police.

ROSIE: It won't be the same ones.

CHRISTINA: What if it is?

ROSIE: They change their beats.

CHRISTINA: What if they haven't?

ROSIE: That was last summer.

CHRISTINA: I saw them, a picture of them, in the paper today.

ROSIE: I saw it, too.

CHRISTINA: They saved a mother's little girl. CPR. She called them heroes.

ROSIE: It's good they saved her girl.

CHRISTINA: Heroes.

ROSIE: They're heroes.

CHRISTINA: Heroes can do anything they want, you know. They give them the key to the city and stuff like that. They could catch us swimming naked and take our clothes and make us leave the water all naked and shine their flashlights on us and hold our clothes above their heads and laugh and say, "Jump." You'll cry.

ROSIE: I will not cry.

CHRISTINA: I won't know what to do. I'll jump and they'll laugh and I won't know what to do. I'll jump.

ROSIE: I promise you, on my honor, I will not cry.

CHRISTINA: What will you do if those heroes come?

ROSIE: I will hide under the weeping willow branches that grace the lake.

CHRISTINA: You said we wouldn't go anywhere near that tree.

ROSIE: I'll swim to the middle of the lake and tread water until they leave.

CHRISTINA: Your legs will tire. You'll drown like the Berridges' boy.

ROSIE: I'm a strong swimmer.

CHRISTINA: They'll come in after you.

ROSIE: They won't get their uniforms wet. It'd tarnish their medals.

CHRISTINA: They could take off their uniforms.

ROSIE: Then they wouldn't be cops.

CHRISTINA: They could take off their medals.

ROSIE: Then they wouldn't be heroes.

CHRISTINA: They could take our clothes and drive away in their police car. Sirens and lights and them laughing.

ROSIE: We'll drive home naked.

CHRISTINA: Our moms will catch us.

ROSIE: They've seen us naked before.

CHRISTINA: What if it's our Dads?

ROSIE: That won't happen.

CHRISTINA: What if it does? Naked? *(Beat.)*

ROSIE: *(In a father's voice.)* "NO MORE SKINNY-DIPPING BEHIND OUR BACKS—SNEAKING AROUND—DOING WHATEVER YOU PLEASE—FOR YOU, YOUNG LADY."

CHRISTINA: Those are your favorite jeans they'd be driving off with. You'd never get them back.

ROSIE: I don't care.

CHRISTINA: Took you two years to break them in.

ROSIE: I'll hide them in a tree.

CHRISTINA: There's only the weeping willow.

ROSIE: I know.

CHRISTINA: They'll find our clothes again and they'll know they've got two naked girls again. And one will shine his flashlight on you and one will shine his flashlight on me. And the water that maybe was like swimming in black velvet when we were alone and moving will be cold when we're still and wondering what to do. And they will order us out and we will be naked and shivering and your tan skin will turn white and frightened. They'll see right into us. Your eyes will fix on them and you won't look at me. You won't tell me what to do and I'll be so cold. They'll say, "Come on out now, girls." And the water will fall away from your body with only hands and wrists, white elbows and arms to cover you. Your arms look breakable. And I'll follow you watching the water run down your back. The flashlights will glare down our faces, down our legs. They'll shine their flashlights one for each of us. They'll smile at us trying to cover ourselves. They'll hold our clothes above their heads and smile at us naked and say, "Jump." And you'll cry and I'll cry and I'll jump.

ROSIE: We'll walk out of that lake like we've got nothing to be ashamed of and we'll look them right in the eye.

CHRISTINA: We won't cry?

ROSIE: We will not cry.

CHRISTINA: When they hold our clothes above their heads and won't give them back and say "Jump"?

ROSIE: We will not cry. You will not jump.

CHRISTINA: When they say with grins on their faces and our clothes in their hands, when they say...

ROSIE: *(Cutting Christina off.)* "Lucky for you."

CHRISTINA: "Lucky for you it was just cops that found you and not some crazy sicko."

ROSIE: "Murderous Peeping Tom."

CHRISTINA: "Rapist."

ROSIE: "What are you two thinking about swimming at this hour with no lifeguard?"

CHRISTINA: "What if a storm came up all of a sudden and lightning struck the lake?"

ROSIE: "Why, you could be electrocuted!"

CHRISTINA: "What are you thinking about swimming with no clothes on?"

ROSIE: "You could catch a chill and die of pneumonia!"

CHRISTINA: "It's cold at night with no sun!"

ROSIE: And when they say, "Run along home now, girls."

CHRISTINA: "Before we call your parents."

ROSIE: We'll just stare at them, but we won't say a word.

CHRISTINA: We won't?

ROSIE: We won't stoop to their talk, talking nonsense. We'll just press them with our knowing eyes and they'll know that we know better.

CHRISTINA: We know all about skinny-dipping at midnight.

ROSIE: Warm, black water, black sky, no flashlights to trash the darkness, one moon, some stars, and a weeping willow tree. A perfectly beautiful night for a swim.

CHRISTINA: Standing there naked we will not cry.

ROSIE: We will not.

CHRISTINA: I can't.

ROSIE: Why?

CHRISTINA: The floorboards creak, they'll wake up.

ROSIE: Tiptoe.

CHRISTINA: My parents have radar.

ROSIE: Climb out the window.

CHRISTINA: There's nothing to climb.

ROSIE: Jump.

CHRISTINA: It's a long way down.

ROSIE: Bend your knees when you land.

CHRISTINA: Catch me.

ROSIE: You're too old for catching.

CHRISTINA: *(Christina climbs into the window frame.)* Just jump and bend my knees?

ROSIE: I don't like to swim alone.

CHRISTINA: It is a beautiful night for a swim.

ROSIE: C'MON JUMP.

(Christina jumps. Lights out.)

END OF PLAY

Waterbabies
by Adam LeFevre

CHARACTERS

LIZ

EMMA

Waterbabies

Lights up. A small office in the newly constructed wing of a YMCA complex in a medium-sized American city. An institutional metal desk with chair, a small couch, a bookcase with a few books for and about children. On the wall, a big daisy made out of construction paper, each petal a different color, each bearing the name of a child—Becky, Andrew, Travis, etc.—and a painting, perhaps a print of a Winslow Homer seascape.

Emma sits quietly on the couch. In her lap lies a swaddled little body. Enter Liz, as if turning from one corridor into another. She holds a scrap of paper in her hand, referring to it as she talks to herself.

LIZ: Right, down the third green hallway. That was the third green hallway. First blue door on the left. Whose left? God, I don't have a clue where I am. Blue door. *(She turns and sees Emma.)* Oh! Hi. Waterbabies? Am I here?

EMMA: He's almost down.

LIZ: Uh-oh. Nap time? Am I late?

EMMA: His eyes are open. I don't know.

LIZ: There was construction everywhere. Central Avenue closed entirely. The arterial backed up to Henshaw. Flashing arrows funneling traffic into one lane. Normally nice people, they get behind a wheel in a situation like that, presto!, swine. Total maniac piglets. And forgive me, this new wing, it's gorgeous, but it's not the "Y" I remember. These color-coded corridors, I cannot fathom.

EMMA: *(Speaking to her bundle.)* No, no. Shh.

LIZ: Ooops.

EMMA: Don't do this to me. It's my life now.

LIZ: I'll whisper.

EMMA: Don't worry. Once he's down, he sleeps like a...like a...lo...like a law.... Damn! Like a lull....

LIZ: Is this bad....

EMMA: Lobster! A lobster. He sleeps like a lobster. There. Bingo.

LIZ: 'Cause if this is a bad time…

EMMA: It's not good or bad, long as it floats.

LIZ: …I could come back. No problem. I've got errands to do, and Jim, my husband Jim's got the baby at home. He takes Wednesday afternoons off now, which is such a blessing. A legitimate breather for me, and he gets his one-on-one Daddy time with Duncan. Am I talking too loud? How old's your little guy?

EMMA: He's… He's about… Oh God, I don't know. You know those days when everything…

LIZ: Boy, do I. I mean, having a kid…

EMMA: Everything is just so…

LIZ: Changes everything, doesn't it?

EMMA: Boneless. Unbraided. Blended in? Something with a *B* in it. *(To bundle.)* Lullaby-bye, Snookums. Sneepytime.

LIZ: What's his name?

EMMA: Oh God. Okay. It's… It's… Lo… Law… Lolaw…

LIZ: It's not important.

EMMA: It's his *name*, for Christsake! I'll get it.

LIZ: Why don't I come back?

EMMA: Blob! No! Bob! Bob. This is my boy, Bob. *(She gently tucks him under the chin.)* Bobby, blobby. Li'l puddin' face. Wow, he's really under now. I'm losing my ambivalence about the immediate future. What is it you want?

LIZ: I called you, remember? I have some questions about Waterbabies.

EMMA: Oh yes. Waterbabies.

LIZ: Just some quick ones, you know, about the philosophy of the time frame, you know. What's developmentally appropriate specifically *vis-à-vis* Duncan, who's pretty advanced, according to our Doctor, physically. It's amazing really. He'll be eleven months next week, and he's *this* far from walking. Because I've read if you wait too long, with some kids—and unfortunately, we only just heard about your program from my friend, Diane, who, by the way, said you just had a *knack* with the little ones. *Enchantress*, in fact, was the word she used. Anyway, I read if you start too late, it can be traumatic and actually instill a fear, you know, of the water and create an obstacle the child then later on down the road has to over-come. If you wait, that is. If you wait too long. Before you start. So, I was just concerned that at eleven months we may have missed the boat, so to speak, with Dunkie. But I don't know, of course. Because this is not…my area. So. *(A pause.)* I guess your Bobby's a waterbaby.

EMMA: It's in the blood.

LIZ: So, how old was he when he started?

EMMA: Oh God, here we go again. Okay, wait. I'll get it. Bob was... When we met he was already nearly this size, so that would make him... It's conceivable he was younger, by a breath or two. Maybe. But you know he's not really mine so none of this is written in stone.

LIZ: Oh. He's adopted.

EMMA: Listen. You hear that?

LIZ: No.

EMMA: He doesn't get that from me. Does your son speak?

LIZ: Oh, yes. Lots of words. Doggie. Horsey. Moomoo.

EMMA: Horsey and Moomoo. Wow. Think I should worry about Bob?

LIZ: No, I mean, well... *How* old is he? No, I mean, no. Each one is just different. Each has his or her own way. Like my sister-in-law's little boy, Wade. He didn't say a word till he was nearly three-and-a-half years old. Then, all of a sudden, one morning, this torrent of language just poured forth from this child's mouth—all these words they had no idea where he'd even heard them, as if they'd been dammed up inside his little brain and finally on this particular day, the dam just burst.

EMMA: This morning I thought I heard him say *waffle*. But he was just choking.

LIZ: Dunkie says *waffo*. And *maypo suppo*.

EMMA: I had to give him a real smack on the back.

LIZ: He calls it *maypo suppo*.

EMMA: Calls what *maypo suppo*?

LIZ: Syrup. Maple syrup.

EMMA: Don't worry. He'll get it.

LIZ: I'm not worried.

EMMA: Bob doesn't talk. He kind of transmits. You gotta stay on your toes.

LIZ: Have you been doing this a long time?

EMMA: What?

LIZ: Teaching infants to swim.

EMMA: Oh. I've been involved in aquatic education all my life. When I was a kid, I tried to teach myself to breathe through my eyes. I just thought I could do it.

LIZ: Aw. That's cute.

EMMA: No, I was absolutely serious about it. I sensed inside me this skill, this ancient, lost skill which I was sure I could salvage from the deep of my memory. I practiced in the bathtub. Kept my mouth and nose just below the surface of the water, and concentrated on bringing air in through my tear ducts, and around my eyes. I never got it. Swallowed a lot of water too. But I learned…that the breath…cannot be contained. It must circulate, always and forever. And that I could not disappear…into what contained *me*…and remain…myself.

LIZ: Wow, so you've really developed a philosophy, haven't you. It's not just the doggypaddle and back-float anymore.

EMMA: The brain is 80 percent water. Does that answer your question? That wasn't your question, was it. Damn. I'm sorry. What is it you want to know?

LIZ: Is Duncan too advanced for Waterbabies? Jim is very gung-ho. I'm just… I may be a little overprotective, I guess. I just don't want anything bad to happen.

EMMA: Well, I don't know then. You see, it's like a dream. In a liquid environment, there are no guarantees.

LIZ: I mean, he's just a baby. I don't want him traumatized. I don't want him set back in any way. As a mother you know what I mean.

EMMA: No. No I don't. You think this is the Marines?

LIZ: No, of course not…

EMMA: Just what do you think I intend to do to little Dunkie?

LIZ: You misunderstand me.

EMMA: Roast him and eat him like a Peking Duck?

LIZ: No, please. I just…

EMMA: Lookit! Ol' Dunkie and me will get along just fine so long as he leaves the *moomoo doggie* out of it. We're swimmers here, not talkers.

LIZ: I'm not worried about *you*. I'm worried about the water.

EMMA: Oh, well. That's different. It is always wise to cast a cold and narrowed eye upon the water. Water can take you places from which, unless you're very careful, there is no return. Places so deep, so quiet, so beautiful, it's more than the human heart can bear. It's always good to pause at water's edge. Hesitation, as they say, is Wisdom's crippled child. For Duncan's sake, let's be perfectly quiet for a moment. No words in the world for a while but water's words.

LIZ: I…

EMMA: Shh! *(There's a considerable pause. Emma cocks her ear toward Bob.)* You hear that? Didn't that sound like *waffle?*

LIZ: I have to talk to Jim.

EMMA: How would he know?

LIZ: About Waterbabies for Duncan. We just have to discuss it a little more before we can make an informed decision.

EMMA: That's a mistake. Men don't trust water. They can't fix it. It eludes them. Not their fault. Just the way it is. Jim'll steer you wrong on this, believe me. The hell with Jim is my advice. Though I'm sure he's an excellent man.

LIZ: We're a team. That's the way we do things. Sorry, I'll just have to get back to you when we decide what to do. Is it the same phone number?

EMMA: I should have told you. There's no space left in this session anyway. All filled up. Just before you arrived a baby crawled in here and formed a complete sentence. Crawled right up into my lap and said, you believe this, without a trace of a lisp or a coo, said, "I shall test the deep." I mean, talk about *advanced*. I was just bowled over by the presence and self-possession of this little fry who couldn't have been more than a handful of moons old. So, I said, "Bless your soul, child, you're in! You're my last water-baby." So, you see, there's just no room. Unless someone drops out. Or drowns.

LIZ: I'm sorry.

EMMA: Maybe next session.

LIZ: Maybe.

EMMA: Or maybe not. Your choice. I'm pro-choice. *(To Bob.)* Don't. Don't. Lullaby-bye. Lullaby-bye.

LIZ: He's waking up?

EMMA: Dreaming. I think he's dreaming. His eyes are open, but he looks very far away.

LIZ: Can I take a peek? I just adore babies.

EMMA: No. No!

LIZ: Okay. Is everything all right? Is your baby all right?

EMMA: Sometimes you have to listen with your feet to hear the SOS from your heart. You don't understand, do you?

LIZ: I'm a mother. Like you. I just want my child to be healthy and happy and safe. That's why I came. That's why I wanted to talk to you. Because I thought you would be able to advise me.

EMMA: I did my best, my level best.

LIZ: Thanks for your time.

EMMA: It was nothing.

LIZ: I hope I can find my way out of here.

EMMA: Just keep turning as the colors change—blue to green, green to yellow,

yellow to red, red to white. At the end of the white there's a big glass door. That's it. That's out.

LIZ: Thanks. Blue to green, *et cetera.* Thanks. Diane, my friend, she says you're an extraordinary teacher. She recommended you. I thought you might like to know.

EMMA: Diane? I don't remember. So many babies, so many mothers. It's hard. I've already started to forget you. It just goes on and on.

LIZ: Good-bye. Good luck with all your waterbabies.

(Exit Liz.)

EMMA: *(She looks down at swaddled Bob.)* Luck. Luckabyebob. I remember it. Like an arrow. The first time I saw you. Flash of silver as you arced in the sunlight. The thrash sending white spray high over the gunnels into my bloodied sheets. Like being struck by an arrow. God. My heart stopped. Then it started beating backwards. I should've thrown you back. I should've thrown you back right then. Now it's too late. I've been struck by your silence. I need to know your secrets. Talk to me. Stop dreaming. Bob? Bob? Say *waffle. Waffle.* Say it. Say *waffle.*

END OF PLAY

After
by Carol K. Mack

CHARACTERS

CINDY: A journalist.
GLYNDA: A fairy.

SETTING

A field near the parking lot in a remote corner of Disney World. It is defined by light. A sense of vast space beyond should house the two actors.

SOUND

Cartoon music, fairy music, munchkin giggles.

After

Precurtain: A medley of cartoon music is interrupted by a loudspeaker announcement.

TOUR BUS DRIVER: *(Voiceover.)* Right over here, folks! That's all, folks! Let's go...time's up. Back on the bus now, boys and girls, we've got *lots* more to see! Hi! Step right up... Hi there. How're ya doin'...everybody here? Aaalll aboard! ... Hello? ExCUSE me, Miss. HEY, you over there? Hello?! We're boarding... Lady?! Hey, you can't go over there! Ma'am... Nobody's *allowed* over there... HEY! Hey *you*, get back here!
(During above, Cindy enters, alert, but casual, then, aware she's off-limits, she runs across stage. She wears baseball cap, jeans, knapsack, sneakers, sunglasses, and ID tag from tour. Cindy is slightly gruff, down-to-earth, independent, bright.)

TOUR BUS DRIVER: *(Voiceover. Very hostile to way out-of-control.)* Somebody get that visitor. She's off-limits! GET HER! GET HER!
(During above noises: Offstage shouts, horns, a bewildered Cindy runs across and flees offstage. Glynda enters, dressed in a Technicolor uniform, and too-high heels, chases her, wobbly. Sparkledust falls in Glynda's wake, then a harp strum as she exits in delicate pursuit. Cindy darts back across, looking behind her, then skids to a stop. The cyclorama lights up and there's a "new dawning" sound as Cindy looks straight out, amazed.)

CINDY: *(Awestruck, looks out to back of house.)* Oh!... WHOA! *(Lowers her sunglasses, removes cap.)* What the...

GLYNDA: *(Sweetly, out of breath.) There* you are!

CINDY: Where?!

GLYNDA: *(Graciously.)* Off-limits, I fear, but...

CINDY: What *is* this *place!?*

GLYNDA: Please come with me now, dear.

CINDY: *(Grabs Glynda's wrist, points to rear of house.)* What's that?!

GLYNDA: What...?

CINDY: Who *are* they?

GLYNDA: Come along, please?

CINDY: They're all over the grass!

GLYNDA: It's not real grass, it's… (*all right*)

CINDY: All over!

GLYNDA: This isn't part of the tour.

CINDY: As far as the eye can see!

GLYNDA: It's not for visitors…

CINDY: *(Confrontational.)* Why not? Why is it "not for visitors"?

GLYNDA: *(Whispering.)* He wouldn't like it.

CINDY: Who?

GLYNDA: Mr. Walt.

CINDY: Walt…? *(Peering at Glynda.)* But he's…

GLYNDA: Yes! But he still *cares.*

CINDY: *(Is she crazy?)* Oh yeah?

GLYNDA: He doesn't like our visitors to be unhappy. Look how upset you're getting. And for what?

CINDY: For what?! You see them? There must be *hundreds* of white horses…

GLYNDA: This is an unscheduled stop and we must disclaim any…

CINDY: *(Finally realizing.) This* is where they all wind up, isn't it?

GLYNDA: *(Simply, Glynda the Good.)* Oh my, oh my, oh my.

CINDY: And all of those couples were princes and…

GLYNDA: *Are* princes. Are! We can't *have* this!

CINDY: *(Into her recorder, a reporter.)* Hundreds of white horses have fallen here along with their riders and they're all gorgeous!

GLYNDA: Oh no!

CINDY: The women are dressed up in *(Squinting.), prom* dresses. Many have blond braids.

GLYNDA: *(Aghast.)* You're a journalist!

CINDY: All the guys are hunks in helmets…

GLYNDA: Forget you saw this please, for your own sake! For your *species!*

CINDY: *(Into recorder.)* They all appear to be smiling expectantly, as if…

GLYNDA: It had to end! Try to understand, it had to end!

CINDY: *(Childlike anger.)* WHY?! It says Happily Ever After!

GLYNDA: *(Brightly.)* That's *right,* dear!

CINDY: That's RIGHT?!

GLYNDA: *(With a sweeping gesture accompanied by stardust.)* Why yes! This *is* Happily Ever After.

CINDY: This is IT? A dump site!? *(To her recorder darkly.)* They're all just *lying* there, thick as penguins, far as the eye can see.

GLYNDA: But happily.

CINDY: You call that happily!?

GLYNDA: Goodness, yes. They're just… *(A rainbow gesture.)* Over.

CINDY: That's not *fair.* *(Cindy unexpectedly bursts into tears.)*

GLYNDA: Go ahead and cry if it makes you feel better! *(Glynda hands Cindy a twinkling handkerchief.)*

CINDY: *(Crying.)* It's… I always thought that *after* was only the Beginning. I thought they'd go a long way after After!

GLYNDA: Oh dear, I know. But you see nothing was written for them.

CINDY: What?

GLYNDA: Just, "The End."

CINDY: *(Explosively ranting.)* That's not fair! After they worked so hard? With the *moats* and the *dragons* and the *towers* and hacking through bramble with *witches* flying after them and does the slipper fit or doesn't it and then *finally* it's all okay and what!? They wind up sprawled all over some stupid theme park in Florida!? That is sick!

GLYNDA: *(Beat, then lamely.)* It's sunny. *(At Cindy's look.)* And you can see they're all quite…content.

CINDY: Forty acres of horses and lovers… *(Thought, turns dismayed to Glynda.)* Oh no! I bet they didn't even… (get a chance.)

GLYNDA: Into the sunset! Hoof beats, anticipation! A brief and shining moment. En route. It does keep them smiling. Forever. *(Lamely.)* Jellybean?

CINDY: I just lost my appetite.

GLYNDA: This isn't an easy job for me either, being a part-time guide here!

CINDY: …You an actress?

GLYNDA: A fairy.

CINDY: *(Flatly.)* A fairy.

GLYNDA: An unemployed fairy.

CINDY: Oh yeah?

GLYNDA: You couldn't tell?

CINDY: No, actually, I never met one before.

GLYNDA: So you think!

CINDY: Right. Do I get three wishes or what?

GLYNDA: That's *genies!* That's what I mean! Fairies are completely misunderstood and it's impossible to find work. A tooth here, a tooth there… *We* are the endangered species nobody talks about. Children ignore our random acts of kindness. Cynics abound. Our forests are cut down and we have nowhere left to go. There are horrible waves in the air from your new-fangled inventions! Oh, how we used to dance to the music of the wind-up Victrola as it wafted gently to the bottom of the garden. And now? We get struck down by words flying through the ether like arrows! "You've got mail!" A million times a night! And what does it *mean* anyhow? *(Disdainfully.)* And the New Age? They've got their angels and their channels but what about us? Nobody cares. You think *you're* disillusioned? I'm disenchanted! I wish I could cry. Fairies can't cry you know. Of course you don't know! Why would you? *(Breaking down.)* Now all I can get is "After!" And it's not even supposed to *exist*. It's strictly Off-Limits...after all these millennia, I'm NOWHERE!

CINDY: I'm really sorry...I don't know what to *say*... *(Looks at her uniform ID tag.)* "Glynda." Should I clap? Would that help?

GLYNDA: That doesn't work. Applause and barking and car horns all scare us to death. And by the way, we hate caraway seeds.

CINDY: Oh. Then, well what can I do?

GLYNDA: Just make up your mind! *(At puzzled look, pointedly.)* Before you get back to the Bus.

CINDY: *(Jolted back to reality.)* Bus.

GLYNDA: *(Coaching.)* Your *Beau* on the Bus?

CINDY: Oh... *(Remembering problem.)* Him. Right.

GLYNDA: Yes *him!* That was why you wandered off, wasn't it?

CINDY: Yeah, I guess it was... It's such a big commitment! I mean I don't know if I can go through with it. I just...

GLYNDA: You must decide!

CINDY: Well, if this is Happily Ever After, you know what you can do with it!

GLYNDA: Well, if you've decided against a wedding celebration, I'll just fade out now.

CINDY: Wait! I, I didn't say that. All I said was I don't *know*...

GLYNDA: Tell me: Does he have a horse?

CINDY: No, they don't ride horses anymore *(With grudging belief.)*, Glynda.

GLYNDA: *(Wistfully.)* Things change.

CINDY: Yes!

GLYNDA: But fairies don't. Neither do fairytales. *(Tiny ping sound.)*

CINDY: *(At ping, small fond smile.)* ...He's got a Jeep Wrangler.

GLYNDA: Ah. *(Tiny ping sound.)*

CINDY: It was really mine and I sold it to him. That's how we met. See I was selling my car to finance a trip to Nepal, and this guy shows up to buy it and then, we wound up going trekking together and, he's really, uh...

(Doesn't say "great," but her recall is positive, romantic.) He's...we've got a lot in common and...y'know he's a journalist too...in fact, he's covering this place...I mean not *this! (Stops abruptly, staring at field, realizing.)* So, you gotta write your own After. That's the deal, huh?

GLYNDA: Exactly!

CINDY: *(Gesturing to field.)* It's gotta be better than...

GLYNDA: *It* could be!

CINDY: *(Getting her point.)* Yeah... It *could* be anything! Right?

GLYNDA: Right! *(A small ping.)*

CINDY: Thank you! You know what? I want to go back now!

GLYNDA: Good! *(As Cindy turns.)* But you can't take anything with you.

CINDY: What do you mean?!

GLYNDA: Memory. We can't let you...

CINDY: Look, I swear I won't print this story, okay?

GLYNDA: It's too dangerous. It would end your species.

CINDY: Okay, okay, but you can't make me forget!

GLYNDA: Don't force me to do anything unkind.

CINDY: Now what are you, a *hit* fairy?

GLYNDA: *(Touches Cindy with wand, immediate effect. Cindy freezes in place. Casts spell with wand.)* Now, forget this field and all tale-spinning, the horse, and all the princes grinning. Forget The End and make a *new* beginning! Forget the pumpkins, the mice, and all witchcrafter, forget it all in love and laughter. Forget, and keep your dream of After. *(Ping.)*

CINDY: *(Opens her eyes, slight disorientation.)* Hello?... I thought I... Excuse me? Where's the bus!?

GLYNDA: It worked! *There* you are, we were just getting worried about you. I'm your tour guide, Glynda?

CINDY: Don't I know you from...?

GLYNDA: The Bus. We must hurry. There's a nice young man on line who's waiting for you...

CINDY: *(Face brightens.)* Oh yeah, *him!* We're getting *married* this weekend!

GLYNDA: How lovely! I'll be there... *(Correcting her slip.)* in spirit.

CINDY: *(Disoriented.)* I feel like, like I forgot something.

GLYNDA: Like a toothbrush? Here. I carry extras.

CINDY: Thanks... Did you see a tape recorder anywhere?

GLYNDA: Is this yours? *(Handing her recorder with tape dangling.)* I think it...dropped.

CINDY: *(As jellybeans fall from tape recorder.)* Where did *they* come from? *(Shaking her head.)* I'm feeling kinda weird.

GLYNDA: *(Steering her away from site.)* Probably something you ate in the cafeteria. Did you eat an apple? Don't worry it's just a spell... Now what did you say your name was?

CINDY: Cindy?

(As they exit.)

GLYNDA: Cindy! Ah, I knew a Cindy once upon a time, long, long ago...

END OF PLAY

Beauty
by Jane Martin

CHARACTERS
CARLA
BETHANY

Beauty

An apartment. Minimalist set. A young woman, Carla, on the phone.

CARLA: In love with me? You're in love with me? Could you describe yourself again? Uh-huh. Uh-huh. And you spoke to me? *(A knock at the door.)* Listen, I always hate to interrupt a marriage proposal, but...could you possibly hold that thought? *(Puts phone down and goes to door. Bethany, the same age as Carla and a friend, is there. She carries the sort of mid-eastern lamp we know of from Aladdin.)*

BETHANY: Thank God you were home. I mean, you're not going to believe this!

CARLA: Somebody on the phone. *(Goes back to it.)*

BETHANY: I mean, I just had a beach urge, so I told them at work my uncle was dying...

CARLA: *(Motions to Bethany for quiet.)* And you were the one in the leather jacket with the tattoo? What was the tattoo? *(Carla again asks Bethany, who is gesturing wildly that she should hang up, to cool it.)* Look, a screaming eagle from shoulder to shoulder, maybe. There were a lot of people in the bar.

BETHANY: *(Gesturing and mouthing.)* I have to get back to work.

CARLA: *(On phone.)* See, the thing is, I'm probably not going to marry someone I can't remember...particularly when I don't drink. Sorry. Sorry. Sorry. *(She hangs up.)* Madness.

BETHANY: So I ran out to the beach...

CARLA: This was some guy I never met who apparently offered me a beer...

BETHANY: ...low tide and this... *(The lamp.)* ...was just sitting there, lying there...

CARLA: ...and he tracks me down...

BETHANY: ...on the beach, and I lift this lid thing...

CARLA: ...and seriously proposes marriage.

BETHANY: ...and a genie comes out.

CARLA: I mean, that's twice in a...what?

BETHANY: A genie comes out of this thing.

CARLA: A genie?

BETHANY: I'm not kidding, the whole Disney kind of thing, swirling smoke, and then this twenty-foot-high, see-through guy in like an Arabian outfit.

CARLA: Very funny.

BETHANY: Yes, funny, but twenty feet high! I look up and down the beach, I'm alone. I don't have my pepper spray or my hand alarm. You know me, when I'm petrified I joke. I say his voice is too high for Robin Williams, and he says he's a castrati. Naturally. Who else would I meet?

CARLA: What's a castrati?

BETHANY: You know…

(The appropriate gesture.)

CARLA: Bethany, dear one, I have three modeling calls. I am meeting Ralph Lauren!

BETHANY: Okay, good. Ralph Lauren. Look, I am not kidding!

CARLA: You're not kidding what?!

BETHANY: There is a genie in this thingamajig.

CARLA: Uh-huh. I'll be back around eight.

BETHANY: And he offered me *wishes!*

CARLA: Is this some elaborate practical joke because it's my birthday?

BETHANY: No, happy birthday, but I'm like crazed because I'm on this deserted beach with a twenty-foot-high, see-through genie, so like sarcastically…you know how I need a new car…I said fine, gimme 25,000 dollars…

CARLA: On the beach with the genie?

BETHANY: Yeah, right, exactly, and it rains down out of the sky.

CARLA: Oh sure.

BETHANY: *(Pulling a wad out of her purse.)* Count it, those are thousands. I lost one in the surf.

(Carla sees the top bill. Looks at Bethany, who nods encouragement. Carla thumbs through them.)

CARLA: These look real.

BETHANY: Yeah.

CARLA: And they rained down out of the sky?

BETHANY: Yeah.

CARLA: You've been really strange lately, are you dealing?

BETHANY: Dealing what, I've even given up chocolate.

CARLA: Let me see the genie.

BETHANY: Wait, wait.

CARLA: Bethany, I don't have time to screw around. Let me see the genie or let me go on my appointments.

BETHANY: Wait! So I pick up the money...see, there's sand on the money...
and I'm like nuts so I say, you know, "Okay, look, ummm, big guy, my
uncle is in the hospital" ...because as you know when I said to the people
at work my uncle was dying, I was on one level telling the truth although
it had nothing to do with the beach, but he was in Intensive Care after
the accident, and that's on my mind, so I say, okay, Genie, heal my
uncle...which is like impossible given he was hit by two trucks, and the
genie says, "Yes, Master"...like they're supposed to say, and he goes into
this like kind of whirlwind, kicking up sand and stuff, and I'm like, "Oh
my God!" and the air clears, and he bows, you know, and says, "It is
done, Master," and I say, "Okay, whatever-you-are, I'm calling on my cell
phone," and I get it out and I get this doctor who is like dumbstruck who
says my uncle came to, walked out of Intensive Care and left the hospital!
I'm not kidding, Carla.

CARLA: On your mother's grave?

BETHANY: On my mother's grave.

(They look at each other.)

CARLA: Let me see the genie.

BETHANY: No, no, look, that's the whole thing...I was just, like, reacting, you
know, responding, and that's already two wishes...although I'm really
pleased about my uncle, the $25,000 thing, I could have asked for $10
million, and there is only one wish left.

CARLA: So ask for $10 million.

BETHANY: I don't think so. I don't think so. I mean, I gotta focus in here. Do
you have a sparkling water?

CARLA: No, Bethany, I'm missing Ralph Lauren now. Very possibly my one
chance to go from catalogue model to the very, very big time, so, if you
are joking, stop joking.

BETHANY: Not joking. See, see, the thing is, I know what I want. In my guts.
Yes. Underneath my entire bitch of a life is this unspoken, ferocious, all-
consuming urge...

CARLA: *(Trying to get her to move this along.)* Ferocious, all-consuming urge...

BETHANY: I want to be like you.

CARLA: Me?

BETHANY: Yes.

CARLA: Half the time you don't even like me.

BETHANY: Jealous. The ogre of jealousy.

CARLA: You're the one with the $40,000 job straight out of school. You're the one who has published short stories. I'm the one hanging on by her fingernails in modeling. The one who has creeps calling her on the phone. The one who had to have a nose job.

BETHANY: I want to be beautiful.

CARLA: You are beautiful.

BETHANY: Carla, I'm not beautiful.

CARLA: You have charm. You have personality. You know perfectly well you're pretty.

BETHANY: "Pretty," see, that's it. Pretty is the minor leagues of beautiful. Pretty is what people discover about you after they know you. Beautiful is what knocks them out across the room. Pretty, you get called a couple of times a year; *beautiful* is 24 hours a day.

CARLA: Yeah? So?

BETHANY: So?! We're talking *beauty* here. Don't say "So?" Beauty is the real deal. You are the center of any moment of your life. People stare. Men flock. I've seen you get offered discounts on makeup for no reason. Parents treat beautiful children better. Studies show your income goes up. You can have sex anytime you want it. Men have to know me. That takes up to a year. I'm continually horny.

CARLA: Bethany, I don't even like sex. I can't have a conversation without men coming on to me. I have no privacy. I get hassled on the street. They start pressuring me from the beginning. Half the time, it never occurs to them to start with a conversation. Smart guys like you. You've had three long-term relationships, and you're only twenty-three. I haven't had one. The good guys, the smart guys are scared to death of me. I'm surrounded by male bimbos who think a preposition is when you go to school away from home. I have no woman friends except you. I don't even want to talk about this!

BETHANY: I knew you'd say something like this. See, you're "in the club" so you can say this. It's the way beauty functions as an elite. You're trying to keep it all for yourself.

CARLA: I'm trying to tell you it's no picnic.

BETHANY: But it's what everybody wants. It's the nasty secret at large in the world. It's the unspoken tidal desire in every room and on every street. It's the unspoken, the soundless whisper...millions upon millions of people longing hopelessly and forever to stop being whatever they are and be beautiful, but the difference between those ardent multitudes and me is that I have a goddamn genie and one more wish!

CARLA: Well, it's not what I want. This is me, Carla. I have never read a whole book. Page 6, I can't remember page 4. The last thing I read was "The Complete Idiot's Guide to WordPerfect." I leave dinner parties right after the dessert because I'm out of conversation. You know the dumb blond joke about on the application where it says, "Sign here," she put Sagittarius? I've done that. Only beautiful guys approach me, and that's because they want to borrow my eye shadow. I barely exist outside a mirror! You don't want to *be me*.

BETHANY: None of you tell the truth. That's why you have no friends. We can all see you're just trying to make us feel better because we aren't in your league. This only proves to me it should be my third wish. Money can only buy things. Beauty makes you the center of the universe.

(Bethany picks up the lamp.)

CARLA: Don't do it. Bethany, don't wish it! I am telling you you'll regret it.

(Bethany lifts the lid. There is a tremendous crash, and the lights go out. Then they flicker and come back up, revealing Bethany, and Carla on the floor where they have been thrown by the explosion. We don't realize it at first, but they have exchanged places.)

CARLA/BETHANY: Oh God.

BETHANY/CARLA: Oh God.

CARLA/BETHANY: Am I bleeding? Am I dying?

BETHANY/CARLA: I'm so dizzy. You're not bleeding.

CARLA/BETHANY: Neither are you.

BETHANY/CARLA: I feel so weird.

CARLA/BETHANY: Me too. I feel… *(Looking at her hands.)* Oh, my God, I'm wearing your jewelry. I'm wearing your nail polish.

BETHANY/CARLA: I know I'm over here, but I can see myself over there.

CARLA/BETHANY: I'm wearing your dress. I have your legs!!

BETHANY/CARLA: These aren't my shoes. I can't meet Ralph Lauren wearing these shoes!

CARLA/BETHANY: I wanted to be beautiful, but I didn't want to be you.

BETHANY/CARLA: Thanks a lot!!

CARLA/BETHANY: I've got to go. I want to pick someone out and get laid.

BETHANY/CARLA: You can't just walk out of here in my body!

CARLA/BETHANY: Wait a minute. Wait a minute. What's eleven eighteenths of 1,726?

BETHANY/CARLA: Why?

CARLA/BETHANY: I'm a public accountant. I want to know if you have my brain.

BETHANY/CARLA: One hundred thirty-two and a half.

CARLA/BETHANY: You have my brain.

BETHANY/CARLA: What shade of Rubenstein lipstick does Cindy Crawford wear with teal blue?

CARLA/BETHANY: Raging Storm.

BETHANY/CARLA: You have my brain. You poor bastard.

CARLA/BETHANY: I don't care. Don't you see?

BETHANY/CARLA: See what?

CARLA/BETHANY: We both have the one thing, the one and only thing everybody wants.

BETHANY/CARLA: What is that?

CARLA/BETHANY: It's better than beauty for me; it's better than brains for you.

BETHANY/CARLA: What? What?!

CARLA/BETHANY: Different problems.

(Blackout.)

END OF PLAY

Off the Rack
by Robert D. Kemnitz and Jennifer McMaster

CHARACTERS

PAULINE

ADRIENNE

Off the Rack

Lights up: A large walk-in closet. The only set piece is a large pole running the length of the stage, crammed with every item of clothing known to woman, hung from one side to the other.

At rise: Pauline is sorting her outfits. In reality she is moving them back and forth with limited results.

PAULINE: Let's see, let's see, long sleeve, long sleeve, long sleeve, short sleeve. Oh, no no no, that will never do. Let's put you over here, no, that's blazers. Blazers and suits. Blazers and suits and skirts. Oh, I remember this one. The look on their faces when I…
(She puts first item back and pulls down a wrap-around skirt, which, as she finds, no longer wraps around.)
Another two weeks at the gym should fix that. Let's see, where was I? Oh, how much time do I have? Damn. Where did that blouse go? Let's see, evening wear—no, that's somewhat-formal wear. Ooh, that's the jacket that goes with the slacks that go with that silk blouse that I wore to my first…
(She pulls down a jacket and tries to close it in front of her.)
Going to have to step up on the Slim Fast. That's fine, that's fine. Let's see, let's see. We have purple, purple, that's almost purple, that's not. Oh, that's the dress—I love that dress.
(She pulls down a dress and tries to pull it over her head. She gets stuck.)
Not even an act of God.
(The doorbell rings.)
She's here! *(Calling from beneath the dress.)* Door's open!
(Pauline struggles to get the dress off her head. After a moment, Adrienne enters. Her movements, dress, and speech are sharp. There is nothing extraneous about her.)
ADRIENNE: Good afternoon. I'm Adrienne Proctor. Proctor Personal Services.
PAULINE: I'm so glad you're here.

(Adrienne reaches to shake hands with Pauline, who reaches out her hand, still holding the dress. Adrienne rips the dress from her hands, whips a plastic garbage bag from her purse, and immediately deposits the dress in the bag.)

PAULINE: My dress—?

ADRIENNE: Let's be clear about one thing. I'm very good, I'm very expensive, and you are paying by the hour. I was told this was an emergency, and I can see now that I was well informed. We're going to have to get to work right away.

PAULINE: Would you like a cup of tea?

ADRIENNE: Never bring beverages near your clothing. *(Adrienne walks past Pauline, directly to the clothing rack.)* I see we've been trying to sort things through ourselves.

PAULINE: I just tidied up a few things.

ADRIENNE: Last-ditch efforts are never a substitute for professional organization.

PAULINE: Well, I just thought I'd—

ADRIENNE: Don't—

PAULINE: —get started so you wouldn't—

ADRIENNE: Organization is not about thought. It's about removing thought. For the next four hours, try to keep from thinking anything. It will make my job much easier.

PAULINE: I'll try to keep that in mind.

ADRIENNE: Marvelous. Okay, Pauline, is it? Right. What is it that you want me to do?

PAULINE: I thought I explained over the phone...

ADRIENNE: Please, say it again. In front of the wardrobe.

PAULINE: I—I don't know what you—

ADRIENNE: Please state exactly the service you wish me to provide.

PAULINE: I...I want you to organize my closet.

ADRIENNE: Louder please.

PAULINE: I want you to organize my closet.

ADRIENNE: Good. It is very important to admit you have a problem. Now don't worry. That was the hardest thing you'll have to do. The rest is up to me. All the hard decisions. So when clothes start crying out to you, just remember—they won't hate you. They'll hate me.

PAULINE: Okay.

ADRIENNE: My motto: Chuck it all and let Goodwill sort it out. Say it.

PAULINE: *(Meekly.)* Chuck it all and let Goodwill sort it out.

ADRIENNE: Good. Now we can get started. You certainly have accumulated a high volume of worthless outfits.

PAULINE: It's a passion?

ADRIENNE: It's a disease. Judging from your stock, you've had the illness a long time. I bet you even keep all your toys and dolls from your childhood.

PAULINE: Of course I do. All of my old Barbie dolls, I must have forty of them—I remember, I had to have every single one of them, as soon as they came out—Malibu Barbie, Tahiti Barbie, Retro Barbie. I had to have them all.

ADRIENNE: Ah, yes. The Barbie Fantasy School of Clothes Shopping. One party, one outfit. Another party, another outfit.

PAULINE: Yes, that's it exactly.

ADRIENNE: Well, some of us were able to select three or four neutral Barbie outfits to mix and match, giving her an endless array of stylish yet versatile ensembles. You see, Pauline, it's not so much what you wear, but how, and in your case, *if* you wear it.

PAULINE: Yes, yes. I see.

ADRIENNE: Let's get one thing straight. I may be brutal, I may appear unfeeling. And I am. And that's what you need.

PAULINE: All right.

ADRIENNE: I have three rules. If you haven't worn it in two months, it gets put aside. If you haven't worn it in six months, it gets considered. If you haven't worn it in nine months, it gets tossed.

PAULINE: You are tough.

ADRIENNE: Yes, I am. Let's have a look at the culprits. *(Adrienne stands at one end of the rack, and begins thumbing through the items. As she thumbs through.)* No, no, no, no, definitely not, no, no, no, fuchsia? I don't think so, no, no, no, no, no, maybe—maybe not, and no.
(Adrienne grabs a stack of clothes off the rack and immediately stuffs them into her trash bag.)

PAULINE: Wait a minute! What are you doing?

ADRIENNE: I'm doing you a favor. *(Looking at the tag of one item.)* Size 6? Please.

PAULINE: I'm on a diet.

ADRIENNE: You and the rest of my clients. May I proceed?

PAULINE: Yes.

ADRIENNE: *(Finding another item.)* Size 8? Still optimistic, are we?

PAULINE: I've been working out.

ADRIENNE: One, two, and lift that twinkie. Let's see, what else do we have? *(Finds another.)* Size 10? Reality begins slowly to set in.

PAULINE: I wore that last year to the Christmas party.

ADRIENNE: And I'm Elle McPherson. Let me guess, you're big boned?

PAULINE: Well, my mother was...

ADRIENNE: It goes. It all goes.

(Adrienne takes another large bundle of clothes and tosses them in the garbage bag.)

ADRIENNE: You've eaten yourself right out of Chanel and into Lane Bryant. *(Adrienne pulls another dress and starts to throw it out.)*

PAULINE: Oh, no. Not that one! Please, anything but that.

ADRIENNE: What is it—your prom dress?

PAULINE: I know I can wear that one again. It's my favorite.

ADRIENNE: And it hasn't fit you since 1985. It goes.

PAULINE: It doesn't!

ADRIENNE: It goes or I go.

PAULINE: *(Pause.)* Okay.

ADRIENNE: Very good. Here, have a cookie. *(Adrienne offers Pauline a cookie from her shoulder bag. Pauline accepts it grudgingly.)* Every time you part with an item of sentimental or other value, you get a cookie.

PAULINE: But why do—

ADRIENNE: If you question me, you do not get a cookie.

PAULINE: Cookies aren't exactly on my diet.

ADRIENNE: Apparently you aren't exactly on your diet, either. Fair?

PAULINE: Fair. *(During the following, Adrienne pulls items off the shelf, looks to Pauline for a verdict, and hands her a cookie at the same time. Then Adrienne tosses the article of clothing.)* Oh, get rid of that one. *(Toss.)* What was I thinking? *(Toss.)* The blue one or the green one?

ADRIENNE: Neither.

(Toss. Toss.)

PAULINE: I was thinking of this one for my promotion interview next Wednesday.

ADRIENNE: What did I tell you about thinking?

PAULINE: Maybe you could make a suggestion?

ADRIENNE: Law firm, right?

PAULINE: Yes.

ADRIENNE: Straight dark skirt, high-neck blouse, cravat, navy blue blazer. You do have shoes?

PAULINE: Other closet.

ADRIENNE: That will be next week.

PAULINE: I don't know where I got all these clothes.

ADRIENNE: Saks, Lord and Taylor, Nordstrom...

PAULINE: I always loved dress-up.

ADRIENNE: Pauline, your dress-up days are over.

PAULINE: I just want to be my own life-size Barbie.

ADRIENNE: If you were a life-size Barbie, you wouldn't be able to stand up straight. You'd have hired a chiropractor, not a Proctor Organizer.

PAULINE: Barbie was the prettiest woman I knew as a little girl. And Ken the handsomest man.

ADRIENNE: *(Holding something up.)* This?

PAULINE: Chuck it. *(She tosses the item herself.)* I had the perfect Barbie wedding planned—it was to be outdoors, in the spring, all my friends were invited, the soundtrack to *Grease* playing in the background and a honeymoon in the Dream House.

ADRIENNE: My Barbie never got married—she couldn't even get a date.

PAULINE: Everything was going to be just beautiful. I'd collected rose petals to spread on the patio, there was a gentle breeze, everyone looked perfect. And Ken stood her up. We waited for hours. No Ken. Barbie was crushed she had her wedding gown on, complete with gold tiara. And Ken just never showed.

ADRIENNE: How awful.

PAULINE: Turns out, Ken had been abducted by my dog Spitfire the night before and buried alive. Buried alive!

ADRIENNE: It's those moments that shape us. Those early traumas. My best girlfriend growing up never had the Crayola 64—she just had the eight fat boring dull colors. To this day, she can't coordinate colors to save her soul.

PAULINE: *(Returning to the rack.)* I wish I had that excuse. I mean, look at this outfit? Seventy-six dollars and just look at it.

ADRIENNE: No. It has a certain rustic charm to it.

PAULINE: Laura Ashley is the demon incarnate.

ADRIENNE: No, really, some of her prints are acceptable.

PAULINE: If you say so.

ADRIENNE: I do. I do. In fact... *(She searches in the garbage bag and pulls out a skirt.)* ...I think I was too quick to judge this one. It has a...*je ne sais quoi*...an appeal. I thought I'd never see this color again, but I've heard rumors that fuchsia is going to make a comeback.

PAULINE: I always thought that was the perfect thing for Valentine's Day.

ADRIENNE: *(Searching through the bag.)* With just a few accessories. Studded belt, oh definitely. Lavender turtleneck. And anklets. Hot pink anklets—that will really turn heads.

PAULINE: Yes! Yes!

ADRIENNE: *(Suddenly dropping clothes.)* What am I saying?

PAULINE: I have some lime green anklets, would that work better?

ADRIENNE: I feel dizzy.

PAULINE: And—dare I say—one of those hippie rope bracelets?

ADRIENNE: Stop! Stop right now! I can't breathe!

PAULINE: Miss Proctor, is everything all right?

ADRIENNE: No, everything is not all right. I've lost my faculties. My fashion senses have left me. I'm too close.

PAULINE: Well, stand over here. It all looks great to me.

ADRIENNE: You don't understand. In my profession, objectivity is everything. I'm losing my discerning eye.

PAULINE: I think you're doing a great job. Let's keep going!

ADRIENNE: I can't see the forest greens for the aquas. I have to get out of here!

PAULINE: Don't go! We're having so much fun!

ADRIENNE: Fashion should never be fun! I have to leave, I must get out of this—this vacuum! I'll recommend one of my associates, I have to leave this place now.

PAULINE: But—?

ADRIENNE: I'm so ashamed.

(Adrienne exits quickly. Pauline is left to her own devices. She looks around the room, heartbroken.)

PAULINE: Well, fine—who needs you.

(Pauline grabs an item off the rack with every intention of throwing it in the bag. But she pauses, looks at it, then places it back on the rack.)

Fuchsia? Well, yes. I think it is about time.

(She reaches for the bag. Blackout.)

END OF PLAY

So Tell Me About This Guy
by Dolores Whiskeyman

CHARACTERS
ANGIE: A woman in her late twenties.
MARLA: Her friend.

TIME AND PLACE
Marla's home. A lazy afternoon.

So Tell Me About This Guy

At rise: Marla and Angie are drinking coffee.

MARLA: Ever try this? *(She produces a bottle of Amaretto and pours a shot into each coffee cup.)*

ANGIE: No.

MARLA: Like liquid almonds. Michael loves it.

ANGIE: Michael? Is that his name?

(Marla snickers.)

ANGIE: Michael. Wow. So—tell me about this guy.

MARLA: *Well.*

ANGIE: Well?

MARLA: *(Laughing.)* Well—

ANGIE: Well???

MARLA: He's so—he's just so, you know.

ANGIE: Uh huh.

MARLA: I mean, he's so, uh, just *so.*

ANGIE: *So?*

MARLA: The way he, when he, how he, that is. I mean he's just *so*—*(A deep breath, slowly exhaled.)*

ANGIE: You're kidding.

MARLA: I mean, sometimes, when he—that is, when we're—I mean, you wouldn't think, just to look at him, but he's really, you know.

ANGIE: Yeah??

MARLA: Like Saturday.

ANGIE: Yeah?

MARLA: After we stopped at Gina's, he took me to the, you know—

ANGIE: Yeah.

MARLA: With the—*(Gestures.)*

ANGIE: Right!

MARLA: And the—(Another gesture.)

ANGIE: Polka band.

MARLA: Right. (Dreamy.) Mmmm.

ANGIE: Yeah?

MARLA: (Too excited to talk.) Well, at Gina's, he was, you know. But after dinner, we—

ANGIE: Yeah?

MARLA: He was just so—I mean so—

ANGIE: Seriously?

MARLA: And then we—well—

ANGIE: (Very interested.) Yeah?

MARLA: You know.

ANGIE: And? So???

MARLA: Well, he's uh. You know.

ANGIE: No.

MARLA: You know.

ANGIE: No.

MARLA: Well, he's. He's. Well.

ANGIE: Is he uh—you know?

MARLA: Pretty much.

    (Angie and Marla giggle explosively.)

ANGIE: Really?

MARLA: Uh huh.

ANGIE: So. Did you uh?

MARLA: No. (She pours more coffee and loads it with Amaretto.)

ANGIE: Oh. But if he's so—you know—

MARLA: Well, he's—shy.

ANGIE: Oh. (Beat.) So where did you—

MARLA: Gina's party.

ANGIE: Oh she's the one who—

MARLA: No, Bob.

ANGIE: Bob was at Gina's? I thought they—

MARLA: They did. But now they're—

ANGIE: You're kidding!

MARLA: Wish I was.

ANGIE: Were they uh???

MARLA: (Nods and snickers.) Uh huh.

ANGIE: (Nods and snickers.) Oh, God.

ANGIE and MARLA: *(Together.)* Feeling no pain!!

ANGIE: Oh, God!

> *(They sip the coffee, fall silent, and grow more serious.)*

ANGIE: Wow.

MARLA: Yeah.

ANGIE: Those two.

MARLA: Those two.

ANGIE: They're like—

MARLA: Yeah. *(Beat.)* All over the kitchen, too.

ANGIE: So what did you—

MARLA: We left.

ANGIE: And where—

MARLA: His place.

ANGIE: And what—

MARLA: Watched a movie.

ANGIE: Movie?

MARLA: Uh huh.

> *(They look at each other and giggle.)*

ANGIE: What kind of movie?

MARLA: A training—training film.

> *(They laugh hysterically.)*

ANGIE: Training film?

MARLA: He's into time management.

ANGIE: Uh, huh.

MARLA: He's—

ANGIE: —Shy. Right. *(She sips coffee, calms herself.)* So how does Bob—

MARLA: From school.

ANGIE: Oh. So he and Bob are both—

MARLA: No, he's an accountant.

ANGIE: Oh.

MARLA: What, oh?

ANGIE: Just oh.

MARLA: Oh as in "oh" or oh as in *oh*.

ANGIE: Neither. Just oh.

MARLA: Accountants can be very exciting.

ANGIE: How exciting?

MARLA: Well.

ANGIE: Well?

MARLA: Well—

ANGIE: Well???

MARLA: Well—

ANGIE: But you haven't?

MARLA: Not yet.

ANGIE: Not that exciting.

MARLA: Well, it's not as if—you know.

ANGIE: So what gives?

MARLA: Nothing.

ANGIE: How long have you—

MARLA: Six weeks.

ANGIE: And still no—

MARLA: He travels. *(An uncomfortable silence.)* More coffee?

ANGIE: So, uh, what did Bob say about—??

MARLA: You know Bob.

ANGIE: I know Bob.

MARLA: That Bob.

ANGIE: That Bob.

MARLA: *(Giggly.)* He's a little jealous.

ANGIE: No!

MARLA: Yeah.

ANGIE: No!

MARLA: Yeah.

ANGIE: Bob has a thing for you??

MARLA: Not for me.

ANGIE: *(It sinks in.)* No.

MARLA: Yeah.

ANGIE: You mean he and—and Bob??

MARLA: In school.

ANGIE: God!

MARLA: I told you he's exciting.

ANGIE: I never knew Bob—

MARLA: You try all sorts of things in college.

ANGIE: But Bob?? He's so—so—so—God, poor Gina.

MARLA: She wasn't there.

ANGIE: Marla—has this guy—and Bob—have you??

MARLA: Come on, Angie. You know Bob isn't my type.

ANGIE: Thank God you haven't—

MARLA: Not yet.

ANGIE: You're not still planning on—

MARLA: Well.

ANGIE: You can't.

MARLA: Actually. I figured—maybe tonight.

ANGIE: You could get a disease!

MARLA: Come on.

ANGIE: How do you know who else he—

MARLA: Hey! Don't talk about him like he's some kind of slut.

ANGIE: Don't you see? That's why he's—shy.

MARLA: Oh, no. It's not that. He really is shy. Even with Bob.

ANGIE: How do you know he'll—

MARLA: He will.

ANGIE: But if he and Bob—maybe he—maybe he—

MARLA: No. He will.

ANGIE: At least make him get a blood test.

MARLA: No time. His flight's due at six.

ANGIE: But how will you—??

MARLA: I'll pick him up at the airport. Bob lent me his van.

ANGIE: With the smoked windows?

MARLA: That's the one.

ANGIE: What about, what about, what about—?

MARLA: No problem.

ANGIE: How will you, how will you—??

MARLA: Trojans.

ANGIE: Oh. Well. Wow.

MARLA: Yeah. (*Thinking of the evening to come.*) Wow.
(*Fade to black.*)

END OF PLAY

Plays
for
Two Men

Guys
by Robb Badlam

CHARACTERS
DUFF
TY

Guys

A booth at McDonald's. Duff and Ty are eating quietly. Both men are in their early twenties. They are reasonably good-looking—Ty somewhat more so than Duff. They are reasonably unkempt—Duff somewhat more so than Ty. Both men are in college. Ty has a newspaper open and is intently scrutinizing it. Duff is staring off, thinking. They munch their fries for a long thoughtful moment. Then a contemplative bite of burger. Repeat. The silent chewing goes on for a bit.

DUFF: You know what I really like, Ty?

TY: What's that, Duff?

DUFF: Breasts.

TY: Sure. *(Pause.)*

DUFF: I mean it. I'm really very fond of them.

TY: Okay. *(Pause.)*

DUFF: Not too big, not too small. Just a good, round breast.

TY: Roundness is key.

DUFF: And firmness. Somewhere between a water balloon and a Nerf ball.

TY: It's important. *(Pause.)*

DUFF: I had a dream once. I was totally naked. Barefoot. Walking through this huge field of naked breasts.

TY: What'd you do?

DUFF: I fell down a lot. *(Pause. Indicates a tray liner or poster with his French fry.)* You suppose Mayor McCheese has much of the hot sex?

TY: Hmm?

DUFF: Mayor McCheese.

TY: Yep.

DUFF: How you figure?

TY: He's the mayor. *(Pause.)*

DUFF: But he's got a big freakish head full of soggy meat.

TY: Never underestimate the allure of celebrity.

DUFF: The allure of celebrity?

TY: Dude, people have sex with Steve Buscemi. *(Pause.)*

DUFF: You suppose anybody ever just goes up to him and takes a big bite out of his face?

TY: Steve Buscemi?

DUFF: Mayor McCheese. I mean, he's a big cheeseburger. You think anybody...you know...bites him?

TY: *(Irritated.)* No.

DUFF: Why?

TY: *(Looking up from his paper.)* Dude. He's the *mayor. (Pause.)*

DUFF: What are you reading?

TY: Crossword.

DUFF: You're *reading* the crossword?

TY: I'm *doing* the crossword.

DUFF: But you're not writing anything down.

TY: I'm doing it in my head.

DUFF: In your head.

TY: Yeah. *(Beat.)* It's pretty hard. *(Pause.)*

DUFF: Why are you doing it in your head?

TY: Lost my pen. *(Pause.)*

DUFF: You could use another pen.

TY: Don't have another pen. *(Pause.)*

DUFF: You could borrow someone else's pen.

TY: I liked my pen. *(Pause.)*

DUFF: You could buy a new pen.

TY: *(Squinting at the page.)* That's a lot of trouble to go through just for a crossword, dude. *(Pause.)*

DUFF: So...you lost your pen and now you're gonna go the whole rest of your life without writing anything down?

TY: It's not much of a plan, but it'll do for now. *(Pause.)*

DUFF: You know what we need, Ty?

TY: Girlfriends, Duff?

DUFF: *(Sighing.)* Yeah.

> *(Ty returns to his crossword. Duff returns to his fries. Suddenly Duff perks up as he notices something offstage. Note: it's important that we never see the young lady in question.)*

DUFF: Dude. Dude. Five o'clock.

TY: My five o'clock or yours?

DUFF: Yours.

(Ty takes a moment to figure out where five o'clock is, then moves to turn. Duff stops him.)

DUFF: Wait! Not yet!

TY: What's the recon?

DUFF: No visible rings. No apparent male accompaniment.

TY: And for lunch…?

DUFF: I believe she's selected the McNuggets.

TY: Solid menu choice.

DUFF: Okay. She's not looking.

(Ty turns, trying not to be obvious but doing a terrible job of it. He tosses a fry over his shoulder then turns to pick it up. He looks in her direction as he retrieves his fry from the floor.)

TY: *(Impressed.)* Zoiks!

(Ty pops the floor fry into his mouth unconsciously.)

DUFF: That is not an unattractive young lady.

TY: Hear, hear. *(Pause.)*

DUFF: You know, if women could spend just half an hour inside a male brain…just half an hour…they'd never talk to us again.

TY: They don't talk to us now.

DUFF: No, I mean all of us. Men. They'd cut us off completely. Because they'd finally figure out that fully one half of the male brain is constantly masturbating. We can't help it. It just happens. It's nature.

TY: Like photosynthesis.

DUFF: Completely independent of our higher brain activities. And it's not just your leering construction workers of the world. It's all guys.

TY: Everybody.

DUFF: Albert Einstein. Probably thinking: E equals MC—I wanna wear your ass for a hat—squared. Couldn't help it.

TY: He's a guy.

DUFF: You're damn skippy. *(Pause.)*

TY: My dad always says he wants to come back in the next life as a woman's bicycle seat.

DUFF: Your dad has some things he needs to work out, dude. *(Pause.)* Ty.

TY: Hmm.

DUFF: She has a pen.

(Brightening, Ty emerges from his crossword.)

TY: My pen?

DUFF: No.

(Ty, disappointed, returns to his crossword.)

DUFF: Ask her if you can borrow it.

TY: But it's not my pen.

DUFF: Dude. Work with me here…

TY: And if it *was* my pen, I couldn't borrow it. You can't borrow things that already belong to you…

DUFF: Dude! This is not about the pen! *(Pause.)*

TY: Oh. *(Pause.)* An "in"?

DUFF: Bingo.

TY: That's a high difficulty maneuver, dude.

DUFF: Opportunity is knocking, my friend. You have an in! You need a pen. She has a pen. It couldn't be more perfect!

TY: Why don't *you* ask her. *(Pause.)*

DUFF: *(Caught, deer in the headlights.)* I don't need a pen. *(Pause.)* Take off your watch.

TY: What?

DUFF: Take off your watch.

TY: Why?

DUFF: So you can ask her what time it is.

TY: Why don't you?

DUFF: I'm not wearing a watch.

TY: *(Trying to make sense of that.)* Eh…Duff…

DUFF: Shut up, Ty.

TY: If you're the one who really wants to talk to her, why do you want me to go over and do it?

DUFF: You'll be my facilitator.

TY: Facilitator.

DUFF: You know. Break the ice. Little small talk. "Say, that's a damn nice pen. Pens are cool. I like pens." Then I join in. "I had a pen once." You get things started. Like a warm-up band.

TY: A warm-up band.

DUFF: Yes.

TY: No.

(Ty returns to his crossword. Duff is eating himself alive. He really wants to talk to this woman, but is powerless to do so. Sensing his anxiety, Ty looks up.)

TY: Just go.

DUFF: What?

TY: Just go over there and introduce yourself.

DUFF: You're real brave when it's somebody else's neck on the line.

TY: What neck? There's no neck. This is a neck-free situation. Worst she can do? Say no.

DUFF: *(Becoming frantic.)* Me? Go over there? Without an in? That's exactly what she *will* do! And where does that leave me? Standing in the middle of McDonald's! Pen-less! Watch-less! And completely emasculated! *(Pause.)*

TY: You've thought about this a lot, haven't you.

(They sit a moment in silence.)

TY: Fifty bucks.

DUFF: Huh?

TY: It's yours. Fifty bucks. You go over there, say: "Hello." She says: "No thanks."…"I have a boyfriend."…"Eat mace and die, freak-boy."…shoots you down in any way—there's fifty bucks in it for you. To soften the blow.

DUFF: Where are you going to get fifty bucks.

TY: I'll sell a kidney. Fifty bucks.

DUFF: *(Considering.)* What if she says yes?

TY: You win a cookie. Dammit man! The real victory is just going over there!
(Pause.)

DUFF: I can't.

TY: Why?

(Duff has no answer.)

DUFF: *(Quietly.)* Because?

TY: Fifty American dollars. *(Pause.)*

DUFF: Fifty?

TY: Fifty. *(Pause.)*

DUFF: And all I have to do is go over there.

TY: Just go over there.

DUFF: And say hello.

TY: And say hello. *(Pause.)*

DUFF: I don't know…

(Ty quietly begins making chicken-clucking noises.)

DUFF: Oh that's not fair!

TY: Fifty bucks.

DUFF: Not enough.

TY: How about fifty bucks and whatever's left of your dignity?

DUFF: Hmm…

TY: *(Returning to his crossword.)* Didn't think so.

DUFF: *(Dander rising.)* Now wait just a minute…you don't believe I can get up and introduce myself to a woman?

TY: Nope.

DUFF: I'll have you know I am very good at making conversation. I have talked to many, *many* women in my life.

TY: Checkout clerks. Waitresses. The occasional telemarketer. *(Beat.)* Mom.

DUFF: Oh, that's it! I will not be mocked. I'm gonna go over there! Oh! I'm goin'! I'm so goin', I'm there already!

(Duff turns away to collect himself. He runs his hands through his unkempt hair. He straightens his flannel overshirt. He checks his breath by blowing into his palm and smelling it. Duff turns back, triumphantly. Ready to go. He stops dead. Pause.)

TY: *(Without looking up from his crossword.)* Gone, isn't she.

(Duff sits. Pause.)

DUFF: You know what I really like, Ty?

TY: Breasts, Duff?

DUFF: Yeah.

(Blackout.)

END OF PLAY

Executive Dance
by Joe DiPietro

CHARACTERS

STEVEN

JONATHON

Executive Dance

A corporate social function. Ballroom-dance music plays.

A dark-suited, middle-aged executive, Jonathon, stands, nursing a scotch and scoping the scene. Another middle-aged executive, Steven, approaches.

STEVEN: Jonathon, hi.

JONATHON: Steven, good to see you. Congratulations on your latest sales figures.

STEVEN: Yes, you saw the memo.

JONATHON: I see every memo. So, some party, eh?

STEVEN: Actually, for a company function, it certainly is lively. So—care to dance?

JONATHON: May I lead?

STEVEN: Go for it.

(Jonathon and Steven begin to rumba together.)

JONATHON: You hear the rumor about Grundig in Marketing?

STEVEN: Promotion?

JONATHON: Into an office with a window.

STEVEN: He doesn't have a window now?

JONATHON: No, he has a couch.

STEVEN: He's gonna have a window and a couch?!

JONATHON: No, he can't take the couch. Another promotion, he gets it back, plus a coffee table.

STEVEN: I thought they downsized Marketing?

JONATHON: Yep, sixty-two heads, not including secretarial.

STEVEN: And Grundig gets himself a window! The suck-up!

JONATHON: That's nothing. Were you in the loop on the rumor about Marmadoski in Finance?

STEVEN: Forced early retirement?

JONATHON: Nope. Gonna give him two windows.

STEVEN: No freakin' way!

JONATHON: I hear whispers he might eventually be the first assistant exec v.p. with a china cabinet.

(Music changes.)

JONATHON: What's this? Fox trot? Wouldn't you know—my weakest step!

STEVEN: No sweat, I'll lead.

(Steven leads Jonathon in a fox trot.)

JONATHON: Uh Steven, I've forgotten: How many windows do you have again?

STEVEN: Jonathon, c'mon! Pretty personal, don't you think?

JONATHON: Steven, are you forgetting who you're dancing with? We started together, slogging through expense reports! We have a bond!

STEVEN: Well—I've got one of those half windows.

JONATHON: I've heard about those.

STEVEN: Yeah, I guess, they didn't want to give me a full window yet, but I certainly didn't deserve no window—

JONATHON: Of course not!

STEVEN: Absolutely! So they gave me half. What about you?

JONATHON: A window. Whole one. And a love seat.

STEVEN: Damn! You know, Jonathon, sometimes I think I don't play the game right! I mean, sure, I haven't been streamlined into an outplaced unit—and thank God, in this economy!—but I look at the lack of furniture and sunlight in my office and I can't help but think...

JONATHON: Wait! Here comes Johnson!

STEVEN: Oh, Jesus! What'd we do?!

JONATHON: All right, all right! Smile and act happy.

(They plaster on smiles and speak to an unseen man, dancing next to them.)

JONATHON: Bill!

STEVEN: Bill! Wonderful function.

JONATHON: Yes! And might I add, having these executive-only dances was a wonderful way of bringing us all together—much better than a softball team. At first, I have to admit, I was a bit skeptical. After all, we have seven women execs and about fifteen hundred men—though I think there's nothing wrong with that, of course—but I believed in your judgment enough to give it a go, and now, I have to admit I find these dances a great stress-reliever. Watch this—dip time.

(He dips Steven, who is not too thrilled but reacts like a good sport.)

JONATHON: See, now, I'm refreshed.

STEVEN: Good to talk to you, Bill.

(They smile and watch Bill dance away.)

STEVEN: You are such a suck-up.

JONATHON: Hey, who's the one sitting in the office with half a window?

(Music changes.)

STEVEN: Oh Christ, a waltz! I have to stop.

JONATHON: Not an option, Steven, not after Johnson acknowledged us. Can't appear as if we're dancing just to get his attention. Don't want to look phony.

STEVEN: I am not an adequate waltzer!

JONATHON: Steven, relax! Calm down. C'mon, just stay in my arms and sway—c'mon—that's right, that's it.

(A moment, as Steven leans into Jonathon's chest and they sway back and forth.)

STEVEN: Did you participate in the last executive-only function: the group spanking?

JONATHON: Don't remind me. So humiliating.

STEVEN: Well, you know what I hear his next executive-only activity is: Twister—

JONATHON: That's not so bad.

STEVEN: —naked.

JONATHON: God! I hope I don't agree to that!

STEVEN: Me neither. I like to think that I have limits.

JONATHON: Hey, hey, who's dancing with Rigatowski from Personnel?

STEVEN: Bittenbauer from Corporate.

JONATHON: Look at those two trying to show off. Pathetic!

STEVEN: I heard they found a dance hall for homosexuals and practiced together. The suck-ups.

JONATHON: Hey, wanna show them how it's done?

STEVEN: What? No! C'mon!

JONATHON: Hey, do you want an entire window and maybe some furniture or what?

STEVEN: Well yeah, still...

JONATHON: Steven, these are tough times. I got a memo about a rumor that they're going to downsize Sales within the next...

STEVEN: What?! I haven't heard that!

JONATHON: Those in the department are the last to know.

STEVEN: What's the consensus hearsay?

JONATHON: Eighty-seven heads, not including receptionists.

STEVEN: Jesus!

JONATHON: Can you mambo?

STEVEN: Not since Club Med.

JONATHON: Follow my hips and be light as a feather! *(Calling off.)* Ramon, hit me with something Cuban!

(Steven and Jonathon break into a vigorous, and rather impressive, mambo. They finish with a flourish.)

JONATHON: They're looking at us funny.

STEVEN: That's 'cause Johnson noticed us. He gave you a smile.

JONATHON: No! Really? A "happy" smile or a "you're-acting-like-an-asshole-so-you're-terminated" smile?

STEVEN: We're about to find out! Here he comes!

(They straighten up and smile as they talk to him.)

STEVEN: Having a swell time, Bill!

JONATHON: And it's so relaxing without the wives around.

STEVEN: Well thank you, we both just like to cut loose once in a while and... Lunch? Four weeks from tomorrow?

JONATHON: How fun!

STEVEN: Yes, we'll call one of your secretaries tomorrow and confirm, right.

JONATHON: How fun!

STEVEN: Bye-bye.

JONATHON: Bye-bye.

(They watch him dance away.)

JONATHON: Score!

STEVEN: What a rush!

(Music stops. They applaud the band.)

STEVEN: *(Warmly.)* So Jonathon.

JONATHON: Steven. I do hope you get the rest of your window.

STEVEN: And I hope you trade up your love seat for an entire couch.

JONATHON: I think we got a future here, pal.

STEVEN: Naked Twister, eh? How bad could that be?

(Steven exits. Jonathon picks up his drink and scopes the scene. Blackout.)

END OF PLAY

Forty-Minute Finish
by Jerome Hairston

CHARACTERS
IKE: A young grocery store clerk.
TERRY: A young grocery store clerk.

SETTING
The present. A grocery store.

Forty-Minute Finish

Two mop buckets. Two mops. Two guys in smocks.

IKE: They're still out there. What the hell could they be talkin' about? The ambulance pulled out of here, what, 7:15. It's like an hour later they're still over there yip yappin away.

TERRY: These things take time I guess.

IKE: I'm trying to make out the words, but their lips are too small. Like trying to make sense out of flapping bologna. Can you make out anything?

TERRY: No.

IKE: C'mon, look for real. Can you read what they're saying?

TERRY: Maybe. I don't know.

IKE: Oh, hold back, man. Don't astound me with the eagle eyes.

TERRY: It's none of our business.

IKE: When the hands are feeling any part of eight o'clock on a Sunday and I'm still sporting this smock, it's totally my business. *(Looking one last time.)* Hell with it, let's just go.

TERRY: Aren't you gonna help me?

IKE: Help you? Help you what? There's nothing left.

TERRY: We might of missed something.

IKE: Let's inspect. *(To the floor.)* What am I seeing? I'm seeing me. I'm seeing you. I'm seeing us. A reflection. The floor's spotless. What's the problem?

TERRY: I don't know. Feels disrespectful. How old do you think that guy was? Sixty? Sixty-five?

IKE: He was old.

TERRY: Exactly my point. He was old.

IKE: Yeah. And old people have strokes, that's what they do.

TERRY: But they usually don't crack their heads open in the process. I mean, you think he's dead?

IKE: I don't know. How would I know?

TERRY: What I'm saying is, people bleed, yeah. But to see it like that. To watch his life spread down the aisle. Somethin' about it. Just didn't seem…Human, you know?

IKE: Well, humans bleed. That's what they do.

TERRY: How can you be like that?

IKE: How am I like, Terry?

TERRY: This is something here. What me and you witnessed.

IKE: We really didn't see anything. He was on the floor before we got here.

TERRY: So, it doesn't bother you?

IKE: What do you want? You want me to squirt a few? I didn't even know the man.

TERRY: You know how long it took to clean up?

IKE: What's that have to do with anything?

TERRY: Forty-two minutes.

IKE: It was longer than that.

TERRY: Forty-two. I checked the clock.

IKE: And you're callin' me distracted?

TERRY: 7:32 we started. First change of water 7:46. Last change eight o'clock. Bringing us up to now. The water's hardly red. Forty minutes. To clean up sixty-year-old blood.

IKE: It was a pain.

TERRY: That can't be possible, right?

IKE: Like a tipped stack of egg cartons.

TERRY: To erase somethin' that old that quick. There's something wrong in that, isn't there?

IKE: You want to give it another once over, what?

TERRY: You're missing the point.

IKE: No, I'm missing the game. And I can't punch out until you do. So if it's going to take us sliding the mop fifty times more, then let's do it.

TERRY: You have to know what I'm talking about.

IKE: What is it we're supposed to do? Turn the clock? Split inside the guy and fix his stroke? We're here to bag groceries. To mop the floors. Not place a Band-Aid on the order of the fucking universe.

TERRY: I just feel we have to own up to the event somehow.

IKE: Did we do it? Did we slam his head into the tile?

TERRY: We cleaned up.

IKE: So that's supposed to tie a knot between us and this guy. You even know this guy's name? I can hardly remember what the man was wearing and I'm supposed to light a candle right here in the middle of the bread aisle.

TERRY: What *was* he wearing?

IKE: Huh?

TERRY: I can't remember what he was wearing.

IKE: Who cares?

TERRY: Somebody does. Somebody's going to want to know what he looked like right before he...you think he's dead?

IKE: Maybe. Who knows. And if he is, what can you do?

TERRY: I could've paid attention. I mean, I would've never noticed the guy at all if he didn't hit the floor. That's all I'm going to remember.

IKE: That's all you can remember. Look, you're tired. You're freaked. But it's over.

TERRY: Yeah. Finished.

IKE: Let's go, huh? We'll watch the game. Throw a few down. Sleep solid. What do you say?

TERRY: Something just won't let me move, you know. Feel like something should be said.

IKE: *(Pause.)* Brown pants. Gray sweater. Baby blue zigzags.

TERRY: What's this?

IKE: What he was wearing.

TERRY: You remember what he looked like?

IKE: Yeah. Black dude. Gray beard. Kinda looked like Grady from *Sanford and Son*.

TERRY: *(Small laugh.)* Get outta here.

IKE: He did. Spittin' image. Almost asked for an autograph when he first stepped in.

TERRY: You know, it is possible. You think it might've been him?

IKE: Nah.

TERRY: Stranger things have been known to happen. You don't think that there's even a chance?

IKE: Nah.

TERRY: You really think he's dead?

IKE: *(Pause.)* Yeah. *(Silence.)* Punch the clock for ya?

TERRY: Sure. *(Pause.)* Some night, huh?

IKE: Some night.

> *(Fade.)*

END OF PLAY

Trying to Find Chinatown
by David Henry Hwang

CHARACTERS
BENJAMIN
RONNIE

SETTING
A street corner on the Lower East Side, New York City. The present.

NOTE ON MUSIC
Obviously, it would be foolish to require that the actor portraying Ronnie perform the specified violin music live. The score of this play can be played on tape over the house speakers, and the actor can feign playing the violin using a bow treated with soap. However, to effect a convincing illusion, it is desirable that the actor possess some familiarity with the violin, or at least another stringed instrument.

Trying to Find Chinatown

Darkness. Over the house speakers, fade in Hendrix-like virtuoso rock 'n' roll riffs—heavy feedback, distortion, phase shifting, wah-wah—amplified over a tiny Fender pug-nose.

Lights fade up to reveal that the music's being played over a solid-body electric violin by Ronnie, a Chinese American male in his mid-twenties, dressed in retro sixties clothing, with a few requisite nineties body mutilations. He's playing on a sidewalk for money, his violin case open before him, change and a few stray bills having been left by previous passers-by.

Enter Benjamin, early twenties, blond, blue-eyed, looking like a midwestern tourist in the big city. He holds a scrap of paper in his hands, scanning street signs for an address. He pauses before Ronnie, listens for a while. With a truly bravura run, Ronnie concludes the number, falls to his knees, gasping. Benjamin applauds.

BENJAMIN: Good. That was really great. *(Pause.)* I didn't...I mean, a fiddle...I mean, I'd heard them at square dances, on country stations and all, but I never...wow, this must really be New York City!
(He applauds, starts to walk on. Still on his knees Ronnie clears his throat loudly.)
BENJAMIN: Oh, I...you're not just doing this for your health, right?
(He reaches in his pocket, pulls out a couple of coins. Ronnie clears his throat again.)
BENJAMIN: Look, I'm not a millionaire, I'm just...
(Benjamin pulls out his wallet, removes a dollar bill. Ronnie nods his head, gestures toward the violin case, as he sits on the sidewalk, takes out a pack of cigarettes, lights one.)
RONNIE: And don't call it a "fiddle," OK?

BENJAMIN: Oh, well, I didn't mean to—

RONNIE: You sound like a wuss. A hick. A dipshit.

BENJAMIN: It just slipped out. I didn't really—

RONNIE: If this was a fiddle, I'd be sitting here with a cob pipe, stomping my cowboy boots and kicking up hay. Then I'd go home and fuck my cousin.

BENJAMIN: Oh! Well, I don't really think—

RONNIE: Do you see a cob pipe? Am I fucking my cousin?

BENJAMIN: Well, no, not at the moment, but—

RONNIE: All right. Then this is a violin, you hand over the money, and I ignore the insult, herein endeth the lesson. *(Pause.)*

BENJAMIN: Listen, a dollar's more than I've ever given to a…to someone asking for money.

RONNIE: Yeah, well, this is New York. Welcome to the cost of living.

BENJAMIN: What I mean is, maybe in exchange, you could help me—?

RONNIE: Jesus Christ! Do you see a sign around my neck reading "Big Apple Fucking Tourist Bureau?"

BENJAMIN: I'm just looking for an address, I don't think it's far from here, maybe you could…?

(Ronnie snatches the scrap of paper from Benjamin.)

RONNIE: You're lucky I'm such a goddamn softie. *(He looks at the paper.)* Oh, fuck you. Just suck my dick, you and the cousin you rode in on.

BENJAMIN: I don't get it! What are you—?

RONNIE: Eat me. You know exactly what I—

BENJAMIN: I'm just asking for a little—

RONNIE: 13 Doyers St.? Like you don't know where that is?

BENJAMIN: Of course I don't know! That's why I'm asking—

RONNIE: C'mon, you trailer-park refugee. You don't know that's Chinatown?

BENJAMIN: Sure I know that's Chinatown.

RONNIE: I know you know that's Chinatown.

BENJAMIN: So? That doesn't mean I know where Chinatown—

RONNIE: So why is it that you picked *me*, of all the street musicians in the city—to point you in the direction of Chinatown? Lemme guess—is it the earring? No, I don't think so. The Hendrix riffs? Guess again, you fucking moron.

BENJAMIN: Now, wait a minute. I see what you're—

RONNIE: What are you gonna ask me next? Where you can find the best dim sum in the city? Whether I can direct you to a genuine opium den? Or do I know how you can meet Miss Saigon for a night of nookie-nookie followed by a good old-fashioned ritual suicide? *(He picks up his violin.)* Now, get your white ass off my sidewalk. One dollar doesn't even begin to make up for all this aggravation. Why don't you go back home and race bullfrogs, or whatever it is you do for—?

BENJAMIN: Brother, I can absolutely relate to your anger. Righteous rage, I suppose would be a more appropriate term. To be marginalized, as we are, by a white racist patriarchy, to the point where the accomplishments of our people are obliterated from the history books, this is cultural genocide of the first order, leading to the fact that you must do battle with all Euro-America's emasculating and brutal stereotypes of Asians—the opium den, the sexual objectification of the Asian female, the exoticized image of a tourist's Chinatown which ignores the exploitation of workers, the failure to unionize, the high rate of mental illness and tuberculosis—against these, each day, you rage, no, not as a victim, but as a survivor, yes, brother, a glorious warrior survivor!

(Silence.)

RONNIE: Say what?

BENJAMIN: So, I hope you can see that my request is not—

RONNIE: Wait, wait.

BENJAMIN: —motivated by sorts of racist assumptions—

RONNIE: But, but where…how did you learn all that?

BENJAMIN: All what?

RONNIE: All that—you know—oppression stuff—tuberculosis…

BENJAMIN: It's statistically irrefutable. TB occurs in the community at a rate—

RONNIE: Where did *you* learn it?

BENJAMIN: Well…I took Asian-American studies. In college.

RONNIE: Where did you go to college?

BENJAMIN: University of Wisconsin. Madison.

RONNIE: Madison, Wisconsin?

BENJAMIN: That's not where the bridges are, by the way.

RONNIE: Huh? Oh, right…

BENJAMIN: You wouldn't believe the number of people who—

RONNIE: They have Asian-American studies in Madison, Wisconsin? Since when?

BENJAMIN: Since the last Third World Unity sit-in and hunger strike. *(Pause.)* Why do you look so surprised? We're down.

RONNIE: I dunno. It just never occurred to me, the idea of Asian students in the Midwest going on a hunger strike.

BENJAMIN: Well, a lot of them had midterms that week, so they fasted in shifts. *(Pause.)* The Administration never figured it out. The Asian students put that "they all look alike" stereotype to good use.

RONNIE: OK, so they got Asian-American studies. That still doesn't explain—

BENJAMIN: What?

RONNIE: What *you* were doing taking it?

BENJAMIN: Just like everyone else. I wanted to explore my roots. After a lifetime of assimilation, I wanted to find out who I really am. *(Pause.)*

RONNIE: And did you?

BENJAMIN: Sure. I learned to take pride in my ancestors who built the railroads, my Popo who would make me a hot bowl of jok with thousand-day-old eggs when the white kids chased me home yelling, "Gook! Chink! Slant-eyes!"

RONNIE: OK, OK, that's enough!

BENJAMIN: Painful to listen to, isn't it?

RONNIE: I don't know what kind of bullshit ethnic studies program they're running over in Wisconsin, but did they teach you that in order to find your Asian "roots," it's a good idea first to be Asian? *(Pause.)*

BENJAMIN: Are you speaking metaphorically?

RONNIE: No! Literally! Look at your skin!

(Ronnie grabs Benjamin's hands, holds them up before his face.)

BENJAMIN: You know, it's very stereotypical to think that all Asian skin tones conform to a single hue.

RONNIE: You're white! Is this some kind of redneck joke or something? Am I the first person in the world to tell you this?

BENJAMIN: Oh! Oh! Oh!

RONNIE: I know real Asians are scarce in the Midwest, but...Jesus!

BENJAMIN: No, of course, I...I see where your misunderstanding arises.

RONNIE: Yeah. It's called "You white."

BENJAMIN: It's just that—in my hometown of Tribune, Kansas, and then at school—see, everyone knows me—so this sort of thing never comes up. *(He offers his hand.)* Benjamin Wong. I forget that a society wedded to racial constructs constantly forces me to explain my very existence.

RONNIE: Ronnie Chang. Otherwise known as "The Bowman."

BENJAMIN: You see, I was adopted by Chinese-American parents at birth. So clearly, I'm an Asian American—

RONNIE: Even though they could put a picture of you in the dictionary next to the definition of "WASP."

BENJAMIN: Well, you can't judge my race by my genetic heritage.

RONNIE: If genes don't determine race, what does?

BENJAMIN: Maybe you'd prefer that I continue in denial, masquerading as a white man?

RONNIE: Listen, you can't just wake up and say, "Gee, I *feel* Black today."

BENJAMIN: Brother, I'm just trying to find what you've already got.

RONNIE: What do I got?

BENJAMIN: A home. With your people. Picketing with the laundry workers. Taking refuge from the daily slights against your masculinity in the noble image of Gwan Gung.

RONNIE: Gwan *who*?

BENJAMIN: C'mon—the Chinese God of warriors and—what do you take me for? There're altars to him up all over the community.

RONNIE: I dunno what community you're talking about, but it's sure as hell not mine. *(Pause.)*

BENJAMIN: What do you mean?

RONNIE: I mean, if you wanna call Chinatown *your* community, OK, knock yourself out, learn to use chopsticks. Go ahead, try and find your roots in some dim sum parlor with headless ducks hanging in the window. Those places don't tell you a thing about who *I* am.

BENJAMIN: Oh, I get it.

RONNIE: You get what?

BENJAMIN: You're one of those self-hating, *assimilated* Chinese Americans, aren't you?

RONNIE: Oh, Jesus.

BENJAMIN: You probably call yourself, "Oriental," right? Look, maybe I can help you. I have some books I can—

RONNIE: Hey, I read all those Asian identity books when you were still slathering on industrial-strength sunblock. *(Pause.)* Sure, I'm Chinese. But folks like you act like that means something. Like all of a sudden, you know who I am. You think identity's that simple? That you can wrap it all up in a neat package and say, "I have ethnicity, therefore I am?" All you fucking ethnic fundamentalists. Always looking for easy answers. You say you're looking for identity, but you can't begin to face the real mysteries of the search. So instead you go skin-deep, and call it a day.

(Pause. Ronnie turns away from Benjamin, starts to play his violin—slow and bluesy.)

BENJAMIN: So what are you? "Just a human being?" That's like saying you *have* no identity. If you asked me to describe my dog, I'd say more than "He's just a dog."

RONNIE: What—you think if I deny the importance of my race, I'm nobody? There're worlds out there, worlds you haven't even begun to understand. Open your eyes. Hear with your ears.

(He holds his violin at chest level, does not attempt to play during the following monologue. As he speaks, a montage of rock and jazz tracks fades in and out over the house speakers, bringing to life the styles of music he describes.)

I concede—it was called a fiddle long ago—but that was even before the birth of jazz. When the hollering in the fields, the rank injustice of human bondage, the struggle of God's children against the plagues of the devil's white man, when all these boiled up into that bittersweet brew, called by later generations, the blues. That's when fiddlers like Son Sims held their chin rests at their chests and sawed away like the hillbillies still do today. And with the coming of ragtime appeared the pioneer Stuff Smith, who sang as he stroked the catgut, with his raspy Louis Armstrong voice—gruff and sweet like the timbre of horsehair riding south below the fingerboard, and who finally sailed for Europe to find ears that would hear. Europe—where Stephane Grapelli initialed a magical French violin, to be passed from generation to generation—first he, to Jean-Luc Ponty, then Ponty to Didier Lockwood. Listening to Grapelli play "A Nightingale Sang in Berkeley Square" is to understand not only the song of birds, but also how they learn to fly, fall in love on the wing, and finally falter one day, to wait for darkness beneath a London street lamp. And Ponty, he showed us how the modern violin man can accompany the shadow of his own lead lines, which cascade, one over another, into some netherworld beyond the range of human hearing. Joe Venuti, Noel Pointer, Svend Asmussen. Even the Kronos Quartet with their arrangement of "Purple Haze." Now, tell me, could any legacy be more rich, more crowded with mythology and heroes to inspire pride? What can I say if the banging of a gong or the clinking of a pickax on the Transcontinental Railroad fails to move me even as much as one note, played through the violin MIDI controller of Michal Urbaniak?

(Ronnie puts his violin to his chin, begins to play a jazz composition of his own invention.)

Does it have to sound like Chinese opera before people like you decide that I know who I am? *(Benjamin stands for a long moment, listening to Ronnie play. Then, he drops his dollar into the case, turns, and exits. Ronnie continues to play a long moment. Then Benjamin enters, illuminated in his own special. He sits on the floor of the stage, his feet dangling off the lip. As he speaks, Ronnie continues playing his tune, which becomes underscoring for Benjamin's monologue. As the music continues, does it slowly begin to reflect the influence of Chinese music?)*

BENJAMIN: When I finally found Doyers St., I scanned the buildings for Number 13. Walking down an alley where the scent of freshly steamed char siu bao lingered in the air, I felt immediately that I had entered a world where all things were finally familiar. *(Pause.)* An old woman bumped me with her shopping bag—screaming to her friend in Cantonese, though they walked no more than a few inches apart. Another man—shouting to a vendor in Sze-Yup. A youth, in a white undershirt, perhaps a recent newcomer, bargaining with a grocer in Hokkien. I walked through this ocean of dialects, breathing in the richness with deep gulps, exhilarated by the energy this symphony brought to my step. And when I finally saw the number 13, I nearly wept at my good fortune. An old tenement, paint peeling, inside walls no doubt thick with a century of grease and broken dreams—and yet, to me, a temple—the house where my father was born. I suddenly saw it all: Gung Gung, coming home from his 16-hour days pressing shirts he could never afford to own, bringing with him candies for my father, each sweet wrapped in the hope of a better life. When my father left the ghetto, he swore he would never return. But he had, this day, in the thoughts and memories of his son, just six months after his death. And as I sat on the stoop, I pulled a hua-moi from my pocket, sucked on it, and felt his spirit returning. To the place where his ghost, and the dutiful hearts of all his descendants, would always call home. *(He listens for a long moment.)* And I felt an ache in my heart for all those lost souls, denied this most important of revelations: to know who they truly are. *(Benjamin sits on the stage, sucking his salted plum and listening to the sounds around him. Ronnie continues to play. The two remain oblivious of one another. Lights fade slowly to black.)*

END OF PLAY

Woozey Woo!
by Robert Macadaeg

CHARACTERS

SALAZAR

AARON

Woozey Woo!

SALAZAR: No no no no no no no. You gotta smooth it. Like this. See? She'll never drink you do it your way. You gotta smooth it past her.

AARON: What? You mean like…?

SALAZAR: No, stupid, like this. Eh? Can't see it, can you?

AARON: Alright.

SALAZAR: Practice a little, get it down.

AARON: Okay okay, I get it.

SALAZAR: You're gonna get arrested your way.

AARON: I said alright! I pour it with my hand like this and it's done.

SALAZAR: No! Not like that.

AARON: What, what?

SALAZAR: Jesus, you're awkward.

AARON: What?

SALAZAR: You can see what you're doing alla way across the room.

AARON: I'm doing it just like you!

SALAZAR: Not even close. Look—watch carefully this time.

AARON: C'mon, no more lessons.

SALAZAR: You gotta do it right!

AARON: I'm gonna do it right!

SALAZAR: You're gonna fuck it up! I ain't goin' down 'cause you're lazy, eh? You wanna complete the purchase transaction you gotta prove to me you ain't gettin' caught in the act.

AARON: C'mon, Salazar—

SALAZAR: Don't c'mon me. Here. Do like this. *(He takes Aaron's hand in his.)* Hold your hand like so; give her something else to look at, do a head-fake—

AARON: No, man—

SALAZAR: You're learning, just go like this—

AARON: This is bullshit—

SALAZAR: Make a diversion, she's gonna look wherever you look—

AARON: I ain't doin' this, Sal.

SALAZAR: You almost got it.

AARON: No. I gotta better way.

SALAZAR: What is it?

AARON: I don't know.

SALAZAR: Forget it, kid. No technique, no sale.

AARON: What are you worried about? I'll think of something.

SALAZAR: Something. What's something? You got something to show me? Eh?

AARON: Yeah. Yeah.

SALAZAR: This talk means nothing to me.

AARON: I'm thinking.

SALAZAR: Think on your own time. *(He makes to leave.)*

AARON: No, no, I know what, I got something hold on alright, just hold on I got something. I got something.

SALAZAR: What?

AARON: I got it I got it I got it. Hold on. I got it. I got something. What if I just, you know, what if, look look look look. Here's what I do. Here's what I do. You listening?

SALAZAR: Yeah yeah yeah…

AARON: Good. Good. Siddown for a second. Okay. What if I just, uh, uh, what if I just wait till she goes to the john?

SALAZAR: What, you mean like when she powders her nose or something?

AARON: Yeah, yeah, when she powders her nose.

SALAZAR: Suppose she don't powder her nose.

AARON: She has to powder her nose.

SALAZAR: Yeah, but suppose she don't?

AARON: She powders her nose!

SALAZAR: Who?

AARON: The chick!

SALAZAR: What chick?

AARON: The chick I'm talking about!

SALAZAR: You got a girlfriend?

AARON: No.

SALAZAR: Then who's the chick?

AARON: I don't know who the chick is! Whatever chick it is that I'm taking out at the time.

SALAZAR: You don't know who the chick is.

AARON: No. It's just some—chick.

SALAZAR: How do you know she powders her nose?

AARON: All chicks powder their nose! It's a thing they do. Chicks powder their nose.

SALAZAR: And you are banking on this.

AARON: What?

SALAZAR: That the chick is gonna powder her nose.

AARON: Look. *(He stands.)* I'm a woman, alright?

SALAZAR: *(Pause.)* Alright.

AARON: I come in. I'm scoping every dame in the place. What kinda clothes they got on, what their dates look like, is anybody wearing my dress. I'm comparing.

SALAZAR: Right, yeah.

AARON: I'm seeing how I stack up against the competition.

SALAZAR: Uh huh.

AARON: I got a mental inventory of everybody in the place, who's with who, the whole shot, just from walking in.

SALAZAR: So?

AARON: So this. I'm walking. I'm taking inventory. All these other broads looking at me, checking me out. This is natural. This is how women work. But this chick, like every chick, this chick that I am with, she maybe has a little confidence problem.

SALAZAR: She's going out with you.

AARON: Whatever. They all got a self-image problem on account of they're fat as cows according to the magazines. Anyway, so I'm this chick, and I start to worry a little. There's some good-looking dames in here. I start to think maybe I didn't floss correctly, I got some spinach stuck in there, or that my fucking nose is shiny—

SALAZAR: Like a shiny nose means shit to a guy.

AARON: That's what I'm saying! It don't! It don't mean shit to a guy, but to a broad, she's not thinking about the guy. She don't give a fuck what you think. She's worried about these other dames and where she is in the food chain. So she goes to the john to check herself out. She looks in the mirror. She powders the make-up that's already there. She accentuates her cleavage.

SALAZAR: Cleavage?

AARON: Yeah.

SALAZAR: What she do to her cleavage?

AARON: She accentuates it.

SALAZAR: With make-up?

AARON: Yeah, yeah, they do it alla time. It's all about highlight and shadow, you know. Like when you draw a sphere or something?

SALAZAR: Yeah?

AARON: Light on the top, dark on the bottom?

SALAZAR: Yeah?

AARON: It's amazing what they do. Fucking out of this world.

SALAZAR: So you slip this chick the mickey while she's in the can painting her tits on.

AARON: Yeah. Good plan, ain't it. *(Pause, he drinks.)*

SALAZAR: You're a punk, you know that?

AARON: What?

SALAZAR: A fucking piker. That's not a plan, there's no art to it.

AARON: Art?

SALAZAR: Yeah. I'm not gonna sell to you.

AARON: What? I gotta be artistic?

SALAZAR: Look. You can't do it the easy way like that. It's rape.

AARON: Rape.

SALAZAR: Yeah.

AARON: It's rape the way I wanna do it.

SALAZAR: Yeah.

AARON: And your way it ain't.

SALAZAR: No, you moron, it's not. Not if you do it right. This is a tool, a facilitator, like being good-looking, or rich, or whatever. Eh? You wanna rape somebody, knock 'em on the head! You're just a freak hangin' out in alleys. But with this—this is your equalizer, your BMW, your six-figure income. You got this you got a beach house. A chiseled jaw. Fancy clothes. You wanna rape, you don't need all that, and I don't want you in my life. Eh?

AARON: Why do it the hard way?

SALAZAR: 'Cause your way you can't justify it.

AARON: But your way you can.

SALAZAR: Yeah. Stupid.

AARON: You're sick.

SALAZAR: You're celibate. *(Pause.)*

AARON: Like this, huh?

SALAZAR: So your hand covers it.

AARON: Like this?

SALAZAR: Right. Look her in the eye. Smile. Charm her a little.

AARON: This is bullshit. I can just get 'em drunk.

SALAZAR: You could do that.

AARON: Yeah, and it's legal.

SALAZAR: Common, but legal, yeah. You been doin' that?

AARON: Yeah.

SALAZAR: And it works?

AARON: Yeah. Kinda.

SALAZAR: Kinda. *(Pause.)* So. How much you want?

AARON: This stuff works?

SALAZAR: Wanna try it?

AARON: What? Right now?

SALAZAR: Yeah. Five minutes you'll be suckin' my dick.

AARON: *(Pause.)* I'll take your word for it.

SALAZAR: Morning comes you won't know what happened.

AARON: Damn.

SALAZAR: That's why you have to do it artfully. Eh?

AARON: Artfully.

SALAZAR: Otherwise it's too easy.

AARON: Too easy.

SALAZAR: The way you sneak it past her is the thrill of the chase.

AARON: Yeah. I guess it is.

SALAZAR: You gotta have that.

AARON: Yeah. Yeah you do.

SALAZAR: You wanna buy some?

AARON: I wanna, yeah. I wanna try it out. First.

SALAZAR: You are right now.

AARON: Right now, yeah. What?

SALAZAR: I did it while you were sitting here.

AARON: I was sitting—I was—

SALAZAR: Another minute you'll be licking my balls.

AARON: You put—you're a freak.

SALAZAR: I'm an artist. *(Pause. Aaron begins to giggle.)*

AARON: You're fucking with me, right?

SALAZAR: Yeah, sure. You're kinda cute, you know that?

AARON: Yeah, well, I got a little something goin' on. Hey!

SALAZAR: What? It's just a compliment.

AARON: Yeah. *(Pause.)* Yeah, I know, I just—I'm kinda woozey.

SALAZAR: Woozey, huh? Woozey looks good on you.

AARON: Huh. Huh. Woooooozey. Huh-huh. That's a funny word.

SALAZAR: Yeah. Heh heh.

AARON: Woozey wooo!

SALAZAR: Hah hah. Yeah. Woozey.

AARON: Woozey woozey woozey.

SALAZAR: Woozey woozey woozey.

(They laugh a little, then are silent. They exchange a look. They burst out laughing again.)

END OF PLAY

Drive Angry
by Matt Pelfrey

CHARACTERS

REX THE MEX: Male, twenties.
CHEMO-BOY: Male, twenties.

TIME AND PLACE

Night in Los Angeles. A thundering '76 Maverick.

Drive Angry

Rex the Mex behind the wheel. Chemo-Boy rides shotgun.

REX THE MEX: Concrete, concrete, concrete...

CHEMO-BOY: My dad stopped by yesterday...

REX THE MEX: ...lights, neon, billboards...

CHEMO-BOY: ...out of nowhere. Just, like, I'm chillin', then KNOCK KNOCK KNOCK, I'm like, "Oh, shit, who's that..."

REX THE MEX: ...rich cars, poor cars, ugly cars, dented cars, cars with tint, cars with out-of-state plates, cars with vanity plates...

CHEMO-BOY: ...so I open the front door and there's my oldster, and he gets in my face, he's like, "How you doin', kiddo?"

REX THE MEX: ...cars with loser zoos, cars with stupid bumper stickers, cars with no bumpers, hot rods, jeeps, vans, busses...

CHEMO-BOY: And I swear to Christ, I almost pass out—his breath smelled like *seaweed*...

REX THE MEX: Asian dudes, Armenian dudes, Arab dudes, black dudes, brown dudes, white dudes...everyone mixing, merging, honking...

CHEMO-BOY: ...like there was this sick, repugnant *stew* brewing in his mouth...

REX THE MEX: Like this freeway is just a big concrete bloodstream full of mechanical germs...angry mechanical germs...

CHEMO-BOY: So he comes in and we talk, same old shit, then he asks me if I've got any soup...and I tell him I got plenty of soup. So now he's there for like, five minutes only and he already wants me to cook for him. So I tell him I got Minestrone and I got Fiesta Bean, but that's not good enough, he wants Vegetable Beef. So I'm like, "Man, just have Minestrone," and so that's what I cook up. So I give him a bowl with some crackers, and he just clams up. Stops talkin'. He just sits there, staring at his soup, brooding. Y'know? Just like, in a funk. This hideous soup-funk. So I said, basically, unless you got money to help me with my medical bills, you can fuckin' get lost. So that's what he did. He split. Didn't touch his soup. Swear to Christ, I wanted to beat him over the head with his prosthetic arm.

REX THE MEX: I know you don't want to hear this, I know you want me to be on your side here and all, but, honestly, your dad sounds like a total fucking stud. I mean, come on! He's all corroded and raspy and tweaked out...

CHEMO-BOY: He's lived in a motel for two years.

REX THE MEX: So? He's a desperate, volatile maverick! He's on the edge!

CHEMO-BOY: But it's by choice...

REX THE MEX: What is?

CHEMO-BOY: His motel lifestyle. He has settlement money from the accident. I know he does.

REX THE MEX: So wait—he's holding out on you? He's got loot?

CHEMO-BOY: I think so.

REX THE MEX: See, *that* I got a problem with.

(They drive in silence for a moment.)

CHEMO-BOY: I hear some scientist in Seattle found Sasquatch hairs...

REX THE MEX: Fuck's a Sasquatch hair?

CHEMO-BOY: Sasquatch is another name for Bigfoot.

REX THE MEX: And some scientist has its hair?

CHEMO-BOY: Well actually, they think they're pubes...

REX THE MEX: Hold on. Sasquatch is covered, head-to-toe, in hair. Correct?

CHEMO-BOY: Yes.

REX THE MEX: Then follow me here: how do you know which hairs are his normal hairs, and which are his pubes?

CHEMO-BOY: When the experts say they got Bigfoot's pubes, you take a statement like that at face value. *(Beat.)* Check it: initial tests show it's definitely some sort of non-human primate.

REX THE MEX: *(Repeating to himself.)* ...primate...

CHEMO-BOY: A primate's an ape.

REX THE MEX: I know what a primate is.

CHEMO-BOY: That's so cool. I hope it exists.

REX THE MEX: Bigfoot?

CHEMO-BOY: Yeah.

REX THE MEX: Why would you give a shit if Bigfoot exists or not?

CHEMO-BOY: I'd hunt it.

REX THE MEX: Get outta here...

CHEMO-BOY: No, man, I would. Chase its ass, blow it away, skin the bastard, make a cool rug. Sell the meat to Burger King or Arby's. *(Pause.)* Can you give me a lift tomorrow?

REX THE MEX: Where to?

CHEMO-BOY: Where do you think?

REX THE MEX: What time?

CHEMO-BOY: Gotta be there by nine.

REX THE MEX: *(Slightly annoyed.)* Yeah, I can give you a ride.

CHEMO-BOY: Hey I don't wanna put you *out* or anything…

REX THE MEX: Just wanted to sleep in.

CHEMO-BOY: So fuck off. I'll find a ride.

REX THE MEX: I'll drive you.

CHEMO-BOY: No, really…

REX THE MEX: …said I'd drive you…

CHEMO-BOY: Hey, you got *sleeping* to do.

REX THE MEX: I said I would fuckin' drive you, okay? Stop sniveling.

CHEMO-BOY: I'm not sniveling.

REX THE MEX: You are. You're sniveling like some kinda *victim.*

CHEMO-BOY: Shut up…

REX THE MEX: Little Chemo-Boy suffering from cancer. Waaa!

CHEMO-BOY: Fuck off.

REX THE MEX: You're not even losing your *hair.*

CHEMO-BOY: What's that supposed to mean?

REX THE MEX: You know what it means.

CHEMO-BOY: No, I don't. Fuckin' tell me.

REX THE MEX: I mean, you know, what kind of wimpy cancer you got that your chemo doesn't make you go bald? You know? On TV, all the cool cancer patients go bald.

CHEMO-BOY: My stuff doesn't do that.

REX THE MEX: …'Cause you got pussy chemo.

CHEMO-BOY: I implore you to fuck off. You're being a dick.

REX THE MEX: I'm chemo for your manhood.

CHEMO-BOY: You're *what?*

REX THE MEX: You heard me. I'm like, chemo for your, whatever, yeah, your manhood. I won't let you become one of those people who start to feed off their disease. My uncle got pancreatic cancer, and that's what he became. Pancreatic Cancer Man. Everything was about his disease. How he's "bravely battling cancer." All that disease hype. The whole time, I'm thinking, what's so fucking brave about battling something you have no choice about? You got cancer. You deal with it. It's like how we treat cops and firemen. They save someone, they catch a killer, and yeah, that's great, but it's their *job.* It's not like some civilian that risks his life to intervene and save someone. A cop or fireman has no choice. Doing that shit is no more than what's expected. It's their job. They're not being heroes, they're earning a paycheck and enjoying a privileged position in society.

CHEMO-BOY: Whatever.

(Pause.)

REX THE MEX: What you goin' in for?

CHEMO-BOY: Like you care.

REX THE MEX: Stop brooding...

(Pause.)

CHEMO-BOY: You ever get a CAT scan?

REX THE MEX: Fuck no.

CHEMO-BOY: Dude, they give you a bottle of this shit, it's like, this white, creamy stuff, you gotta drink it before going in, so your insides will show up when they take the picture...

REX THE MEX: ...yeah...

CHEMO-BOY: ...stuff, I'm not kidding, is like drinking *moose semen.*

REX THE MEX: ...not that you know what drinking moose semen is like...

CHEMO-BOY: I'm using poetic imagery so a puny mind like yours can grasp the horror and complexity of what I'm saying.

REX THE MEX: I think I appreciate that.

CHEMO-BOY: You fuckin' better.

REX THE MEX: So...

CHEMO-BOY: ...so that's what they're doing tomorrow. I'm drinking a pint of moose cum, then they're shooting iodine into my veins to find out if I got any creepy shit hiding out.

REX THE MEX: That's fucked up.

CHEMO-BOY: Yeah it is ...

(Pause. Rex the Mex thinks about something.)

REX THE MEX: Let me ask you a question. Let me pose a thought to you...

CHEMO-BOY: Please do.

REX THE MEX: Why did you get cancer?

(Slight pause.)

CHEMO-BOY: I don't know.

REX THE MEX: But what did the doctors tell you?

CHEMO-BOY: It could be any one of five hundred reasons.

REX THE MEX: But at your age, ass-cancer is rare.

CHEMO-BOY: Extremely.

REX THE MEX: So why did this shit grow inside of you?

CHEMO-BOY: I just told you—I don't fuckin' know.

REX THE MEX: Yeah? Well I *do*.

CHEMO-BOY: Oh, great.

REX THE MEX: I do, man. I really do.

CHEMO-BOY: There is no way on God's green earth you know anything my doctors don't know.

REX THE MEX: What you continually fail to grasp, my diseased little friend, is that I am not burdened by over-education. I haven't spent eight years after high school getting taught how to think and what pre-packaged crock of shit to spout so that I appear smart at parties and espresso bars. I actually think. I have forced myself to remain open to the Cosmic Whatever.

CHEMO-BOY: "The Cosmic Whatever?"

REX THE MEX: That's right…

CHEMO-BOY: Alright—what's your diagnosis?

REX THE MEX: Existential pollution.

CHEMO-BOY: What the fuck is that?

REX THE MEX: All the shit out there. All the shit that pisses you off and eats at you day in and day out. All that shit has crawled up inside your ass and died like a sick rat. And that got everything infected.

CHEMO-BOY: And the shit is…?

REX THE MEX: Well, as I touched on already—the chicks that piss us off, our bullshit jobs, our fucking parents and especially the psychotic, selfish, assholic drivers who plague us every day of our lives. You see, all these elements are out there, like secondhand smoke—like *smog*—it's drifting, hanging in the air, contaminating our world. That's why our enforcement, our roadway counter-offensive against the scumbag fuckers of the world—that's why it's so important.

CHEMO-BOY: Hmmm…

REX THE MEX: Am I right? You know I am.

CHEMO-BOY: It's food for thought.

REX THE MEX: It's a fucking all-you-can-eat buffet and it's all true.

CHEMO-BOY: Yeah. It is.

REX THE MEX: *(Something grabs his attention.)* Here we go…

CHEMO-BOY: Where?

REX THE MEX: Next lane over.

CHEMO-BOY: Red truck?

REX THE MEX: Uh-huh.

CHEMO-BOY: What's the crime?

REX THE MEX: Merges like an a-hole, then cut across three lanes of traffic without signalling.

CHEMO-BOY: That is totally unacceptable behavior.

REX THE MEX: Agreed. *(Rex accelerates. Chemo-Boy produces a pellet handgun from under the seat.)* How's the pellet supply?

CHEMO-BOY: Doin' okay.

REX THE MEX: We need more?

CHEMO-BOY: We're cool.

REX THE MEX: Just tell me when.

CHEMO-BOY: I know the game.

REX THE MEX: Anyone behind us?

CHEMO-BOY: No.

REX THE MEX: Don't do it until just before the next off-ramp.

CHEMO-BOY: Who do you think you're talking to?

REX THE MEX: We can't get careless.

CHEMO-BOY: Don't worry about it.

REX THE MEX: Here it comes...

CHEMO-BOY: It's time to administer some real medicine. Chemo for a tumorous city...

REX THE MEX: Concentrate on the job at hand.

CHEMO-BOY: Shut up. I am. Here we go.

(Chemo-Boy leans out of the window, aims the pellet gun, fires three shots. Rex turns the steering wheel sharply toward the off-ramp. Glass shatters. Tires squeal. Blackout.)

END OF PLAY

Game Theory
by Peter Sagal

CHARACTERS

MARK

PAUL

Game Theory

Two men in business suits, Mark, mid-twenties, and Paul, mid-thirties, stand on either side of a line drawn on the ground.

Long pause. They look at each other.

MARK: Let me see if I understand this game…

PAUL: What's to understand?

MARK: I just want to say it out loud, so we both understand.

PAUL: What's to understand?

MARK: Why don't you explain it, then?

PAUL: You have to convince me to step over the line. I have to convince you to step over the line.

MARK: Why?

PAUL: To teach us negotiating skills.

MARK: That doesn't make any sense.

PAUL: Sure it does. It's just a game.

MARK: What are the rules? Games have rules.

PAUL: No rules; just the arbitrary goals. I get you to come over to my side, you get me to come over to your side. Thus we learn the skills of negotiation and persuasion.

MARK: But it can't work. I mean, I gain nothing by going over to your side of the line. That's not negotiation, negotiation you have to offer something. Mutual benefit.

PAUL: Okay. I'll buy you lunch if you come over here.

MARK: Oh, come on.

PAUL: Really.

MARK: That's not negotiation, that's bribery.

PAUL: Like you said, there are no rules. Just results.

MARK: "You Are the Bottom Line."

PAUL: What?

MARK: The motto of the camp.

PAUL: I didn't know.

MARK: They got it written on the gate. In the grill work.

PAUL: Come on, what do you say, huh? Step over the line, I'll buy you lunch.

MARK: How do I know that you will?

PAUL: Because I'm a nice guy. I keep my word. Ask anybody.

MARK: Nobody here to ask. Everybody else is on the Trust Tower, dangling each other on ropes.

PAUL: Then you'll just have to trust me.

MARK: Besides, getting a free lunch has got nothing to do with the game. If I cross over the line, I lose the game.

PAUL: So?

MARK: So that's the point, isn't it? Not to lose.

PAUL: I thought you thought the game didn't make any sense.

MARK: Maybe not, but that's why we're here, to play the game. There's something to learn here.

PAUL: You know my boss sent me here.

MARK: So did mine.

PAUL: My boss is very eager to see how I do.

MARK: I don't think anybody is going to grade us. This is supposed to improve our interpersonal business skills, our sense of self.

PAUL: Well, if my sense of self doesn't improve significantly, it's going to be out of a job. So what do you say?

MARK: I think you're worried too much. It's just a game. There are lessons to be learned if you win or lose.

PAUL: So let me learn from winning. Then we can share our insights.

MARK: No, wait. Let's be logical about this. What are they trying to teach us?

PAUL: To figure out how to win.

MARK: What would be the point of that?

PAUL: Winning.

MARK: Winning what? How often in business do you have to convince someone to step across a line?

PAUL: It's a metaphor.

MARK: Right. For what?

PAUL: I don't know, for quarterly sales; tell you what, I'll buy you dinner, too.

MARK: All the meals are included. Low fat and nutritious.

PAUL: Then when we get out.

MARK: We're going about this the wrong way. We've got to think like the people who put us here. They're consultants. Corporate management consultants, right?

PAUL: Yeah.

MARK: How do they pitch this to our Vice President of Human Resources? Send us your junior execs, and for five thousand a head we'll teach them to cross lines?

PAUL: It's possible.

MARK: So the question is, how does our Human Resources veep think? An oxymoron, I know, but still. Remember when he put one of these kitten-hanging-from-a-twig posters in every single cubicle? "Hang in there?"

PAUL: What's your point?

MARK: That there's something Soft and Cuddly here. Something warm. Hidden beneath the apparent cold binary cruelty of a win-lose situation. They want to teach us something. How to think outside the lines—as it were.

PAUL: Tell you what—I'll just give you cash. Buy your own dinner when you're back in the world. Get something with cream sauce. Something with meat, for God's sake.

MARK: I don't eat meat. I like the food here.

PAUL: If you don't cross, I'll punch you. I'll tear you limb from limb!

MARK: You'd have to cross the line to get at me. And then I'd win.

PAUL: You're a lousy businessman! You couldn't sell water in a drought!

MARK: What are you doing now?

PAUL: I'm trying to provoke you into attacking me. Then you have to cross the line.

MARK: No good. I study Zaiki-chuan, it's this progressive martial art where we learn to simply ignore all attacks.

PAUL: Look—how old are you?

MARK: What does that have to do with anything?

PAUL: The game. Trust me.

MARK: Twenty-five.

PAUL: So is everybody. You're all twenty-five, twenty-six, couple years out of college or business school. I'm thirty-five; hanging around you people I feel like Humbert Humbert.

MARK: Humbert who?

PAUL: Never mind. The thing is, you're all here to get started. I'm here because I've tried everything else. It's my *job*, do you understand?

MARK: What is your job, by the way?

PAUL: Vice President of Human Resources.

MARK: Oh. Sorry.

PAUL: It wasn't always this way. I was like you, they put me in sales, dangled those year-end bonuses like meat on a stick and we all bayed and yapped and went at it. But I wasn't any good, you know, they gave us this crap to sell and I knew I didn't want any and I couldn't think of why anybody else would.

MARK: I see.

PAUL: No, you don't! You're young, you think anything's possible, you've always been brilliant, you've always been picked first, you think it's never going to end! But it will, it will. The last VP of Human Resources just vanished one day. Didn't even clean out his desk. They told me to take his place and I felt a cold wind. Now I sit there, and I order kitten pictures, or pictures of marathon runners and sunsets, with these slogans: "Go the Distance." "Talent Is No Guarantee of Success." But what is? There aren't any posters that tell you that!

MARK: Hey—calm down, okay? It's just a game.

PAUL: It's not! It's my life! I'm sitting there one day, wondering when it's going to be my turn to vanish, and I find the brochure for this place. "Executive Boot Camp," it says. "Send your managers to our wilderness to teach them to survive in yours." And the testimonials! The skills, the confidence! Rapelling down cliffs without a care in the world! It's what I needed. I wrote up a memorandum right away.

MARK: Well—thanks. I'm really enjoying it.

PAUL: This is my last chance. Don't you see? You're young. What does it matter to you to lose this game? It's everything to me. Please. Come across the line. Let me win. *(Pause.)*

MARK: That's not necessary.

PAUL: Yes it is, I just told you—

MARK: No. I mean for either one of us to win. Or lose. We can both win.

PAUL: Are you crazy? It's one line. Two sides. One winner, one loser.

MARK: Sure. That's what it looks like. But they're trying to teach us to think laterally. If the choice is apples or oranges, we're supposed to think—tutti frutti.

PAUL: I don't follow.

MARK: The rules say, you win if the other person crosses the line. But they don't say, only one person can win.

PAUL: You mean—

MARK: We both cross the line, at the same time. We both win.

PAUL: That doesn't happen in real life.

MARK: We don't expect it to happen. That's what they're trying to teach us. Cooperate to achieve all your goals. I can see that on a poster, can't you? *(Pause.)*

PAUL: Hmm. We cross at the same time?

MARK: Exactly. Then arm in arm we go off to lunch. It's couscous with roasted chipotle peppers today; I can't wait. *(Pause.)*

PAUL: This is supposed to make us better executives?

MARK: Better people. Count of three?

PAUL: Okay. I count, though.

MARK: Deal.

PAUL: One, two, three. *(Paul crosses over. Mark takes a step but does not cross.)*

MARK: Two out of three?

(Fade to black.)

END OF PLAY

Plays
for
One Woman and One Man

The Blue Room
by Courtney Baron

CHARACTERS

SAILOR

WOMAN

The Blue Room

Lights up. The middle of the South Pacific, coordinates: 48° 30'S/125° 30'W. A blue room rocks steadily, twilight casts shadows of waves on the walls. A Woman in a blue slip lightly drags her finger in a blue tub of water, moving a tiny blue toy boat. A Sailor kneels on the upper deck of his ship, looking out into the ocean. He scrubs the deck with a brush. He remembers the Woman, she remembers nothing but the moment of his memory.

SAILOR: She dreams of me.
    (The Woman dreams.)
SAILOR: She loves the water.
    (She puts her feet into the tub and smiles.)
SAILOR: She loves the water, I think sometimes she may be a seal. I can picture her smiling, lips pulled back and I see her teeth, her gums are fleshy like salmon, I think sometimes she is a seal.
    (The Woman pours water into the tub.)
SAILOR: What do you love?
WOMAN: *(Reacting to the water in the tub.)* Water.
SAILOR: She comes to the locks to watch the ship come in. When the salmon spawn they get caught in the locks and seals congregate because the catch is easy, like pink gold. They swat and catch enough to be full in an hour. We men try to keep them at bay but they always return. It's like trying to keep a kid out of a candy store. She says something, something that would make anyone fall in love, but really she just says...
WOMAN: *(As if she heard a noise.)* Hello?
SAILOR: And I can't help myself because she would make a good catch for any man. And I don't know anything about her before the ship comes in and we're married before I set sail again. She dies while I'm away and I remember her into the sea. And without knowing it, she's trapped in the blue room where we spent our first night together. I trap her there with too much remembering. And as the tale goes, the sailor who remembers love too strongly, who thinks of her too hard will find nothing but the

woman trapped in the memory, out to sea, in the middle of the sea. Too far for anyone to swim safely and there are no seals out here.

(The Sailor jumps ship. He lands on the periphery of the blue room.)

SAILOR: Just the blue motel room. And she tells me she loves the water, and I tell her I will have to leave and she tells me she married me because she loves the sea and wants me to take her along. But I can't and she tells me I'm her last chance. And I say that chance is never worth depending on and when I leave in the morning, she spits and says that she will get there one way or another. And so she does. Because she is well versed in the game of memory. In the lore of sailors. And in the middle of the sea she gets what she wants without begging. And I sail for money, because it is a job. Because the ocean is only the traveling—land is the arrival. And she loves the water. She loved me, maybe. Married me, to be out at sea, where land is a memory, I think she is a seal. *(The Sailor enters the blue room.)*

WOMAN: Here is my sailor.

SAILOR: She is my wife. *(The Sailor slides into the tub. The Woman giggles.)*

WOMAN: I'll give you a bath, it's what a dirty sailor needs, wash the grit. *(He kisses her and she shies away.)* Look what I've brought you! *(She holds up the toy boat.)* For my sailor! Tell me about the sea. *(He tries to kiss her again. She laughs and splashes him.)*

SAILOR: Come here.

WOMAN: Tell me about the boat, the sails…

SAILOR: It's cold and lonely and smells of fish.

WOMAN: Ha! My sailor!

SAILOR: We spend the days barefoot, socks mold to our feet if we leave them on while we work.

WOMAN: You've made the sea here, taste the water. From the salt between your toes. *(She washes him with a cloth in the tub.)*

SAILOR: You can't drink sea water.

WOMAN: I know of a place where you can, just where it feeds into the Amazon, off the coast of South America, in the Atlantic a hundred miles before the shore, the water there is fresh, you must have been there.

SAILOR: No.

WOMAN: No?

SAILOR: No.

WOMAN: I would go there and drink the ocean. Like the story of the five Chinese brothers, all identical, with different talents. The first brother could swallow the entire ocean. Hold it all in his mouth. Full and smiling. I would be full and smiling if I drank the ocean.

SAILOR: You would dehydrate and die.

WOMAN: Have you ever washed behind your ears?

SAILOR: I'll buy you a house. You can fill it with flowers.

WOMAN: Buy me a boat. I'll be happy then.

SAILOR: There are no flowers on boats. It's bad luck to bring them aboard. Nothing grows there but moss and longing.

WOMAN: My father was a farmer, the only thing he grew was dirty root vegetables, potatoes and turnips. He died and I said I would never grow a damn thing. So, I came to coast, everything is under the surface of the water... I never learned to swim and the first time I saw the sea I knew I didn't need to know how.

SAILOR: You have to swim, to be a sailor, you have to.

WOMAN: My father found nothing but bitterness in the ground.

SAILOR: When I'm at sea, do you know what I think of?

WOMAN: Freedom?

SAILOR: Land. All day I look out to see hard dry earth. I crave it. I've gotten to where sand won't do, I prefer grass, hard dirt. I miss mud. Clean things. A woman to hold onto. *(He pulls her in close.)*

WOMAN: But at night, do you follow the stars?

SAILOR: Sure.

WOMAN: And see the red meteors?

SAILOR: Mostly we see nothing. Just waves and more waves. The night, the day, the day, the night, the clouds and flying fish. I'm getting out.

WOMAN: What?

SAILOR: Of the bath. Come to bed.

WOMAN: But the water is just right.

SAILOR: Why did you pick me?

WOMAN: Pick you?

SAILOR: A whole crowd of us and you came up to me.

WOMAN: Get back in.

SAILOR: You're beautiful. *(He stands up, dripping wet, he pulls her close. He looks her in the eyes, she looks above him and then grabs one of his hands.)*

WOMAN: Your hands are like barnacles.

SAILOR: Sailing is my trade, only a job.

WOMAN: Funny, my father's hands were like potatoes, eyed with calluses. *(He finally kisses her hard and she goes limp. He lays her down.)*

SAILOR: Barnacles make cement, stick to anything they touch, won't let go.

WOMAN: And you won't let go.

SAILOR: In the morning.

WOMAN: Take me with you.

SAILOR: I can't.

WOMAN: I want to live on the ocean.

SAILOR: I'll be back. You have the ring, my promise.

(She pulls away, stands, back to the Sailor.)

WOMAN: Do you know that there is gold in the sea? I want that. I want to be a sailor.

SAILOR: You're a sailor's wife.

WOMAN: I will follow you.

SAILOR: You'll make us a home. We'll have children to keep you company.

(He hovers over her and kisses her. He starts to undress her.)

WOMAN: I picked you because I could smell it on you, see it in your watery eyes, I knew that you would love me enough to want—

SAILOR: I want you on the shore.

WOMAN: —to take me with you.

SAILOR: I became a sailor because I had nothing to come home to. And if you come with me, what then?

WOMAN: You'll be home. *(The Woman pulls away.)*

SAILOR: No. It moves too much. No matter what you've heard, everyone gets sick. You'd get sick. All of that damned back and forth, everything gets lost. Your sense of taste, of smell. Everything. And your skin never feels right.

(They exchange a look, the Woman seems to resolve something, she falls back into the Sailor's arms.)

WOMAN: Then you'll dream of me and I will follow you.

(The Sailor closes his eyes. He returns to the deck of the ship and resumes his scrubbing. He speaks while the Woman does the following: The Woman returns to the position she was in at the start of the play. She replays her movements from the beginning until the point of the Sailor's entry: The Woman dreams. She puts her feet in the tub and smiles. The Woman pours water into the tub.)

SAILOR: The night, the day, the day, the night, the clouds and the flying fish. She died the afternoon I left. They sent word and I dreamt of her. I put her out to sea. And at the point in the South Pacific where land is farthest away on both sides, the blue room appeared. I passed it once, I knew she was there. But she is stuck in the memory and doesn't know that I have given her a home on the open sea. Rocking back and forth. Her skin is slick now from the mist and waves. Her hands are like nothing and I try to remember her differently, give her something else, to let her know that I have given her the sea and I have no reason to touch land again. I think maybe she is a seal, stuck in the blue room where we spent our wedding night. And it floats there. *(The Sailor jumps, the sound of splashing water.)*

WOMAN: Here is my sailor.

(The Sailor slides into the tub. The Woman giggles.)

WOMAN: I'll give you a bath, it's what a dirty sailor needs, wash the grit. *(He kisses her and she shies away.)* Look what I've brought you! *(She holds up the toy boat.)* For my sailor! Tell me about the sea. *(He tries to kiss her again, she laughs and splashes him.)*

END OF PLAY

Creep
by James Christy

CHARACTERS

ANNE

HOOVER

Creep

Anne is on a cell phone at a party. She paces as she talks and plays with her jacket, which is on a table in front of her. On the other side of the stage Hoover sits on a couch, his arm draped over the side holding a beer. He is eavesdropping. Each time she looks in his direction he pretends to be reading a magazine on his lap.

ANNE: You think I'm enjoying myself? My jacket *is* on and I've been giving her dirty looks since we got here. I know they are... I know, they're not going to be waiting on me, I told you... No, not right this second, I told her I'd give her a half hour, she's got ten more minutes. I don't know, she thinks if I leave without her it'll be too forward. *(Confidentially.)* You don't even know. You have to see her tonight. She's worse than usual...kissing this guy's ass and laughing at things that aren't even close to funny... It's the same shit... I know... I know, and then she wonders why they make her miserable... *(Looking at a spot across the room.)* I don't know, pretty much what you'd expect. Well, first of all he's really short so she towers over this one even more than usual, which is embarrassing right off, you know...but the main thing is he's just so boring... No, not really, but you don't have to talk to him, you can just tell, he's got it all over his face. All over his clothes. He's just mediocre, you know, he can't help it. *(She looks around, a bit quieter.)* They all can't, it's like they've all been dipped in it. Alright, now I'm being mean... *(She turns around and sees Hoover, lowers her voice, and faces the other way.)* I think one of them's kind of looking at me, if you don't hear from me in an hour call 911. Alright, eight minutes. Love you too.

(She hangs up. Hoover looks at her for a beat then looks away.)

HOOVER: Who do you know?

ANNE: What?

HOOVER: Who do you know who do you know who do you know? Here, at the party, who do you know?

ANNE: No one. I'm, uh, a friend of a friend. I'm really just waiting for someone.

HOOVER: Uh huh. Do you want me to introduce you around? I can introduce you to some people.

ANNE: No thanks, I'm not really feeling so well.

HOOVER: Really? Huh. I'm sorry to hear that.

ANNE: I'm fine, I'm just not feeling too social. *(Pause.)*

HOOVER: You see that guy over there?

ANNE: Which one, the guy with the purple jacket?

HOOVER: No not that fuck, the guy by the sink.

ANNE: Yeah?

HOOVER: He's got Kurt Cobain's pancreas.

ANNE: What?

HOOVER: *(As he swigs his beer.)* No shit. Cobain's pancreas.

ANNE: Why?

HOOVER: I don't know, he's always had this fucked-up pancreas, some genetic thing, and he needed a new one, and for a long time he was on this waiting list because they're hard to come by and he wasn't, like, on the brink or anything. But one day his doctor called him up and told him to bring his ass in for surgery. He didn't know it was Cobain's pancreas until like two days later. He hadn't even heard Cobain was dead yet, this candy striper chick comes up to him when he wakes up and goes, "Dude, you're so lucky, you got Kurt's pancreas." And he's like, what the fuck, and she's like, "Yeah, don't tell anyone I told you, I could get in trouble, it's supposed to be confidential."
(Beat.)
Can you imagine that shit? To wake up and find out A that Cobain's dead, and B that you've got his fuckin' pancreas? Jesus Christ.

ANNE: But wouldn't it be... I mean, he was like a heroin addict wasn't he? Can they just give them out when they're—

HOOVER: That's what I thought, but it was cool. Apparently his liver and his stomach linings were all fucked up but his pancreas was fine.

ANNE: And he's okay now? Your friend?

HOOVER: He's not my friend. I think he's kind of a dick actually, but yeah he's alright. He's not supposed to drink anymore, but he does anyway and nothing's happened to him yet. Can't listen to Nirvana though.

ANNE: Jesus.

HOOVER: *(Pause. He points to another side of the room.)* And do you know Brock?

ANNE: I told you I don't know anyone.

HOOVER: The guy with the beard?

ANNE: *(Warily.)* Yeah?

HOOVER: He's a stuntman, right? And he got booked for like four weeks of work on the *Phantom Menace.* So it's like his third day and he has this scene where he fights with Ewan McGregor and they were rehearsing it on the set; I guess he hit McGregor too hard 'cause he got all pissed and tried to really fight with him, and Brock is like a black belt and he had him in a headlock in like five seconds, right? So after they separated and McGregor cooled down he came back over to Brock and said he was sorry and acted like they were just buddies blowing off steam. But after lunch one of the A.D.'s came up to Brock and told him he was fired. And now he's like blacklisted from working on movies because it totally ruined his reputation. What a dick. Guy was just doing his job, you know?

ANNE: *(Bewildered.)* Yeah.

HOOVER: And you see that guy on the stairs? He's got this totally boring job answering phones at this Internet company. And he'd been there like a year and a half, and they went public and he had all these stock options, and the stock went crazy and he made like two and a half million dollars. He can do whatever he wants now, but he hasn't quit, he still does that same shitty job, lives in the same shitty apartment—

ANNE: *(Interrupts.)* Wears the same shitty clothes...

HOOVER: He still acts like he has no money because he feels that with money he'll lose his identity. Without money he was a loser, he was used to that, he knew what it was, he did it well. Now if he starts to enjoy his money he thinks he has this huge potential to fuck it up somehow, to lose it or get it ripped off, you know? It makes sense when you think about it.

ANNE: *(Beat. She looks at him, he looks down.)* No, no it doesn't make sense. That makes no sense. In fact, that sounds like bullshit. It is, isn't it? It's bullshit.

(He tries to contain a smile.)

It's all bullshit, isn't it? That guy doesn't have Kurt Cobain's pancreas, and that asshole isn't a stuntman either. You're just full of shit, aren't you?

(He laughs.)

What is your problem?

HOOVER: So, what's your problem with Liz?

ANNE: What? How do you know her name?

HOOVER: I don't think he looks boring, he seems cool enough to me.

ANNE: You heard that? You were listening to me?

HOOVER: And as for kissing his ass, I think she's just being polite, you know. There's nothing wrong with that.

ANNE: So what, you've been fucking spying on me?

HOOVER: To me it looks like you're jealous.

ANNE: Jealous of Liz? Jealous of Liz because she's talking to some zombie broker from New Canaan?

HOOVER: So why are you so angry with her?

ANNE: First of all I'm not, second of all if I was it's just because I'm stuck here in this hole talking to you when there's somewhere I'm supposed to be.

HOOVER: And you don't care enough about her to want her to meet someone and be happy?

ANNE: You think she's going to be happy with him? If he ever calls her after tonight. *Big* if. And if they go out a few times and can stand each other, and even if they even get married and have beautiful fucking kids, he will never make her happy.

HOOVER: Why not?

ANNE: Because she'll always be thinking that she could have done better. Found someone more interesting, better looking, funnier. Taller. You don't understand.

(Looking at her.)

She used to do really well, guys liked her, people liked her, she was fun. And then somehow she just…lost something. She doesn't have the same confidence or self-respect, I don't know. You can see it, you know, look at her, she looks ready to be wounded.

HOOVER: That's called vulnerable.

ANNE: So? Vulnerable means you look like you're about to get your ass kicked. Why is that good?

HOOVER: Why is that bad?

ANNE: It's not bad, it's just pathetic, I think. It's not a quality I'd want to advertise.

HOOVER: What do you want to advertise?

ANNE: I don't want to advertise anything.

HOOVER: If you had to describe how you'd like to be seen.

ANNE: I don't know. You tell me.

HOOVER: Like you've got your shit together.

ANNE: Uh huh. But I don't…

HOOVER: I just think you're bored. Bored with your life, bored with yourself, bored with that guy on the phone. I think you feel like nothing different happens to you anymore and everybody looks the same and nothing really matters to you or excites you like it used to.

ANNE: *(Lets this sink in for a second.)* Is that so? Well listen, it's been a pleasure listening to your bullshit stories about people you don't know and your bullshit pop psychology about people you've just met but I really have to get going. *(She starts to get up.)*

HOOVER: They're not talking anymore.

ANNE: What?

HOOVER: He's talking to some other girl now. She went into the bathroom.

ANNE: Great. He made her real fuckin' happy.

(He looks at her and shakes his head.)

What? What are you saying? I don't care? What the fuck do you know? She's my fucking friend, it's my shoulder she's going to be crying on, I'm the one who'll listen to her and tell her it's gonna be okay, that he wasn't worth it anyway.

HOOVER: I didn't say that.

ANNE: *(Getting upset.)* What then? What? Do I have problems? Yes. Do I sometimes take them out on other people and be a bitch on the phone? Maybe. What the fuck business is it of yours? You don't know me, you don't know my friends.

HOOVER: I didn't say any of that.

ANNE: *(Almost shouting.)* So what, then. What are you saying?

HOOVER: *(Rattled.)* Nothing. I'm not saying anything. *(Pause.)* Listen, do you, do you want a beer?

ANNE: What?

HOOVER: Beer. Do you want a beer?

ANNE: *(Calming down.)* Uh, no. No thanks.

ANNE: *(He gets a cooler out from under the table in front of him, opens a beer for himself.)* What's that?

HOOVER: My cooler.

ANNE: Yeah, I can see it's your cooler, why do you have a cooler? Why a cooler? You're at a party. It's not a picnic, there's a refrigerator here.

HOOVER: *(Shaking his head, he's been down that road before.)* Uh huh, that's not for me. The fridge at a party? No way. Doesn't work, someone always gets screwed. I'm happy to b my own b, but it's gonna stay my own b, you know?

ANNE: But you offered me a b.

HOOVER: Hey, I'll give away all my b, I'm not stingy, but if I give it away, I want to know where it's going, you know? I don't know these people, I don't want them in my stuff.

ANNE: You said you'd introduce me around, you must know somebody.

HOOVER: Nope.

ANNE: Well who'd you come with?

HOOVER: No one. I live down the street, I heard some people talking about a party and thought I'd check it out.

ANNE: So you know no one here.

HOOVER: No one.

ANNE: *(Beat.)* So you're basically trespassing?

HOOVER: I wouldn't call it that.

ANNE: What would you call it?

HOOVER: I don't know, hanging out.

ANNE: No, it's not even hanging out. It's hovering. You're undermining the whole purpose of the party. You're the anti-party. You're like a one-man wrecking crew. I mean parties are supposed to be social events, right? Well what do you do exactly? You sit here by yourself, completely isolated. *(She picks up his cooler from under the table.)* Protecting your cooler of beer—

HOOVER: *(Interrupts.)* I offered you a beer.

ANNE: —You make up stories in your head about these people you don't know, and you eavesdrop on people's conversations. *(Beat. She rests her case.)* Am I right?

HOOVER: *(Trying not to be defensive.)* I don't know. Basically.

ANNE: *(A beat, she opens a beer and sits back on the couch considering this, trying it for herself. She nods her head and looks at him, then back at the party.)* I could see that.

(She takes a swig. He smiles. Blackout.)

END OF PLAY

After You
by Steven Dietz

CHARACTERS

AMY: A woman in her early thirties.
BEN: A man in his early thirties.

SETTING

The present. A chair in a room in an American city.

A song to be used as a possible musical frame around the play is Bob Dylan's "Most of the Time" from the album *Oh Mercy* (CBS Records, 1989); however, producers of this play are hereby cautioned that permission to produce this play does not include rights to use this song in production. Producers should contact the copyright owners directly for rights.

After You

Amy sits in a simple wooden chair. She wears a white cotton robe. On the ground in front of her is a basin of hot water, a mug of shaving cream, and a straight razor. Nearby, a single white candle burns. Ben stands near Amy. He wears jeans, boots, and a white T-shirt. He has a white towel draped over his shoulder. They stare at each other for a long time.

AMY: I'm cold.

BEN: You'll be fine.

AMY: Ben, I'm—

BEN: You'll put your feet in, and it'll—watch, I'll show you—
  (Amy sits in the chair.)

BEN: There, now put your—

AMY: *(Having put one foot in the water.)* Aaaaauuuuugggghhhhh.

BEN: That's good, right?

AMY: It's—

BEN: Other foot.
  (She puts her other foot in, stifling her impulse to scream.)

BEN: Right? That's good. *(He applies shaving cream to her legs after warming them with a wet towel.)*

AMY: Ben?

BEN: Hmm?

AMY: To what do I owe this?

BEN: It was a thought I had. *(Silence.)* You want me to go?

AMY: No.

BEN: This would have been one of my regrets.

AMY: You have a list?

BEN: You have a problem with that?

AMY: Just fishing. *(Silence.)*

BEN: I always wanted to do this. Fair?

AMY: *(Stares at him.)* Fair. *(Silence.)*

BEN: Bend.
  (She bends her legs as he shaves a bit.)

BEN: Yes. It's on the list. I don't leave things—do I? You know this. I don't—

AMY: It's an obligation.

BEN: I didn't—

AMY: That's you to the quick. See it through to the—dot the i's, cross the t's, no matter what, no matter the carnage, no matter if the getting there is fruitless or wrenching or—

BEN: Do you want this or not? *(Silence.)*

AMY: Ben?

BEN: Fruitless?

AMY: Look.

BEN: Wrenching? *Please.*

AMY: Ben, wait—

BEN: I don't need to do this. I don't have this—there is not this *thing* welling up in me that says *do this*, okay? I don't need to do this, Amy. I really don't.

AMY: Fuck you. *(Silence.)*

BEN: Say again?

AMY: You heard me.

BEN: Yes. *(Silence.)*

AMY: *(Smiles a bit.)* Yes?

BEN: Yes. *(He begins to shave her legs.)*

AMY: I shaved you once. Do you remember?

BEN: I'd forgotten that.

AMY: Are you paying me back?

(Ben starts wiping some of the cream off her legs.)

AMY: Ben—

BEN: I'm remembering now.

AMY: What are you doing?

BEN: I'm taking the cream off your legs. I'm shaving you without the cream.

AMY: Why?

BEN: I'm paying you back.

AMY: How was I to know your face was that sensitive?

BEN: Maybe the blood.

AMY: What're you—ouch, careful.

BEN: Maybe the blood should have been a warning.

AMY: Right.

BEN: A sign. Blood is a sign. Watch blood.

AMY: It was harder than I thought. It looked so easy every morning when you did it.

BEN: Straighten.

(She straightens her leg, he reapplies the cream.)

BEN: Thank you.

AMY: The slope of it, you know, the landscape—

BEN: You thought you knew my face.

AMY: I thought I knew your face.

(She is touching his face. He takes her hand away, gently, and continues shaving her.)

AMY: Do you have these written down?

BEN: These—

AMY: These things. This list of obligations. You what, over time you go home and check them off? Then one day you're done owing me? One day I'm a clean slate?

BEN: This is shit you found charming, this is—

AMY: I never found—

BEN: What, now you—

AMY: I never found that charming. I never did.

BEN: Be bigger, Amy. Be bigger than that. Admit that my—

AMY: Your *what?*

BEN: My scrupulousness—

AMY: Ha.

BEN: That my sense of detail, my noting and crossing off of tasks was a charming thing to you. A thing you used to call *concern.* And a thing you have since *renamed,* a thing you now—

AMY: Manipulation.

BEN: See, yes, now you have renamed it. And, no, I don't have them written down. I can stop, okay? I don't need to do this. I wanted to see you, but if you'd rather pretend that each other is dead or something, then—

AMY: Ben. It's me. Save breath. I know you know how this is. You missed a spot. I know you know this is nice. *(Silence. He shaves her.)*

BEN: You in love?

AMY: Have you been waiting to hold a razor to me and ask me that?

BEN: I don't miss your sarcasm.

AMY: You might.

BEN: It's been a year. I don't.

AMY: You will.

BEN: I might.

AMY: No.

BEN: You're not?

AMY: I'm not.

BEN: C'mon. Nobody?

AMY: I didn't know we'd be graded on this.

BEN: I'd like to be.

AMY: In love.

BEN: Yes. I'd like to know who's after you. I'd like to have that settled.

AMY: Is there a line forming?

BEN: I definitely won't.

AMY: What?

BEN: Miss your sarcasm. Hold still.

AMY: Don't begrudge me my jealousy. I like my jealousy. It keeps me close to you.

BEN: I'll tell you about jealousy: I resent people who encounter you. Checkout clerks you hand money to. Waiters who bring your wine and French fries. Strangers who share your elevator and ride to your floor even though it's five floors out of their way.

AMY: You're the only one who ever did that.

BEN: I resent Jehovah's Witnesses who come to your door. They get you without caution. They get you straight ahead.

AMY: And you get?

BEN: I get judgment and longing.

AMY: Well, that's what's left.

BEN: I don't believe that. *(Silence. He shaves her.)* We were at a dinner party for one of your publishers, we didn't really know anyone there. Do you remember this?

AMY: When?

BEN: A year ago.

AMY: Keep going.

BEN: We sat at opposite ends of the table, not saying a word, and a man that neither of us knew looked at us, and said: You two must have a delicious secret. *(He looks at her. Silence.)*

AMY: I remember.

BEN: You got shy.

AMY: Yes.

BEN: It looked good on you.

AMY: I've been trying to remember the last moment when it was still lovely. I think maybe that was it.

BEN: It didn't change in a moment, Amy. It didn't all—

AMY: Of course not. I'm just saying there was a point (I believe this, I do), there was a point when it began to *turn*. A point before the screaming and the lies. Before counseling and jealousy and dividing up our friends. And the moment before that point was still innocent, still lovely. At that moment we still wanted to show each other off. *(He wipes her legs with a wet towel. She touches his hair, pulls him closer to her. They kiss. They part.)*

BEN: Who's after me?

AMY: Someone…reminiscent.

BEN: Of what?

AMY: Of who I thought you were. Fair?

BEN: Fair.

AMY: And ditto I would guess?

BEN: Ditto.

AMY: It's all misdirection and faulty theories. All we really want is to find someone we are certain to dazzle. *(Silence. He closes her robe, covering her legs.)*

BEN: This completes our mission.

AMY: Stay for a glass of wine.

BEN: You replaced the glasses we broke?

AMY: It's been a year.

BEN: Thanks.

AMY: But?

BEN: I'd love to.

AMY: What, you've got a date.

BEN: Yes. Jealous?

AMY: Where are you—wait, *may I?* Where are you going on this date?

BEN: My house.

AMY: Brazen of you.

BEN: I thought so.

AMY: And who is—wait, *may I?* Who is the lucky victim?

BEN: A three-hundred pound blind piano tuner named Delmore. I've been trying to get this piano tuned for a year. He'll be at my house at six. Sorry.

AMY: You have a piano now?

BEN: Yes.

AMY: Pets?

BEN: Fish.

AMY: Fish?

BEN: I'm working up to pets. How 'bout a raincheck?

AMY: Hmm?

BEN: On the drink.

AMY: That's you to the quick. I'll let you know. Fair?

BEN: Yes.

AMY: Okay.

BEN: Great word, fair.

> *(He puts on his jacket, prepares to leave. Long silence.)*

BEN: Be well.

AMY: I'd like to see your piano. Some month or other.

BEN: I don't have a piano. You know that.

AMY: I know that. *(Silence.)*

BEN: Ben?

AMY: Hmm?

BEN: There's blood on my leg.

AMY: Watch blood. Blood is a sign.

> *(Ben looks at her for a moment, then exits. Amy sits in the chair and begins rubbing lotion on her legs as the lights slowly fade to black.)*

END OF PLAY

The Individuality of Streetlamps
by Anna K. Gorisch

CHARACTERS

MELISSA: A woman in her twenties.
ANDY: A man in his twenties.

SETTING

The front porch of a house. A summer evening. There is a porch swing, but it is not hanging.

The Individuality of Streetlamps

At rise: Melissa is sitting on the porch. She is sipping a beer, and is a little dressed up. Andy walks up to the porch.

ANDY: Hey there.

MELISSA: Hey. To what do I owe this honor?

ANDY: Oh, I just got off work, thought I'd drop by. What's with the outfit?

MELISSA: What do you mean?

ANDY: You look nice. Are you heading out soon?

MELISSA: No, I just got home from work.

ANDY: Is that what you wore to work?

MELISSA: Yeah? So?

ANDY: You wore that to a day-care center?

MELISSA: It's not a day-care center, it's a summer school for the arts.

ANDY: If you say so. It just doesn't seem like the right outfit to play with kids in.

MELISSA: I just wanted to look nice.

ANDY: You do. You look nice. You know I always loved that dress.

MELISSA: Yeah, I remember. *(Pause.)* You want a beer?

ANDY: Sure, thanks.

MELISSA: I'll get you one. *(She doesn't.)*

ANDY: So, how is the new job?

MELISSA: Good. Tiring. The kids are great. They wear me out. It doesn't pay enough. The usual.

ANDY: Good, I'm glad to hear it. At least I'm not the only one who's under-appreciated.

MELISSA: Not hardly.

ANDY: What happened to the porch swing?

MELISSA: It fell.

ANDY: I can see that. Why? *(He goes over to inspect it.)*

MELISSA: I don't know. Maybe I've put on weight.

ANDY: Christ, were you in it?

MELISSA: Unfortunately.

ANDY: Are you okay?

MELISSA: Yeah. I got a couple of bruises, but I'm okay.

ANDY: What were you doing?

MELISSA: I was swinging.

ANDY: Vigorously?

MELISSA: I guess.

ANDY: Well, whatever you were doing must have been intense. I don't think this can be fixed. You'll have to completely rehang the thing.

MELISSA: I wouldn't begin to know how.

ANDY: Then it looks like you're swingless. I don't think I can fix it. These things aren't made for swinging, you know. They're made for sitting.

MELISSA: I know. I don't want to talk about it, okay?

ANDY: Okay. *(Pause.)* What's with the streetlamp?

MELISSA: Hmmm? Oh, I don't know. It never really comes on and stays on. It just sort of flickers.

ANDY: Huh. I wonder why.

MELISSA: I have no idea, but it's been like that since I've lived here.

ANDY: Funny that I never noticed it before.

MELISSA: I guess your focus was elsewhere.

ANDY: Yeah, I guess it was. *(Pause.)*

MELISSA: So, how's Amanda?

ANDY: She's good. She just got a new job downtown.

MELISSA: I bet it pays good.

ANDY: Unbelievable. She's got this huge office, big window, access to the company beach house in Florida, the works.

MELISSA: Must be nice. I can't complain, though. I have access to the company crayon box.

ANDY: Right on. And the kids are great, right?

MELISSA: Oh, yeah. They're something. There's this one kid, Jason. He cracks me up. He's got this killer creative energy, and he's so focused. He's a lot of fun.

ANDY: What's his last name?

MELISSA: Stewart.

ANDY: Oh yeah. That's Barbara's kid.

MELISSA: Who's Barbara?

ANDY: Amanda's stepsister.

MELISSA: Well, hot damn, you're relatives.

ANDY: Yeah, in a sense. Barbara's brought her kids to a couple of family cookouts and stuff. Is he the one in middle school?

MELISSA: Yeah, he'll be twelve next month. I figure I'll make cupcakes or something. I hope I have one just like him someday.

ANDY: You really do like this kid.

MELISSA: Sure I do, he's great. He's so serious. Today he told me he would be leaving early. I asked him why. He said he had to go take care of something. He said it like he, I don't know, he had a meeting with his financial advisors or something. He's so cute.

ANDY: Oh my God.

MELISSA: What?

ANDY: I don't believe this.

MELISSA: What?

ANDY: You've got a crush on this kid.

MELISSA: Oh for God's sake…

ANDY: You do, you have a crush on an eleven year old!

MELISSA: Oh, come on, he'll be twelve next month.

ANDY: He's not even a teenager.

MELISSA: I don't have a crush on him! That's completely ridiculous.

ANDY: Do you think about him when you're off work?

MELISSA: Yeah, sometimes.

ANDY: Got any pictures of him?

MELISSA: I got pictures of all the kids.

ANDY: Does he show up in your dreams?

MELISSA: Once I had a dream I was babysitting him, but so what? That doesn't mean anything.

ANDY: Sounds like you've got all the classic signs.

MELISSA: He's just a great kid.

ANDY: Come on Mel, you can be honest with me. How long have you known me?

MELISSA: A long time.

ANDY: So?

MELISSA: Okay, so he makes me wish I was ten again. Things were so much simpler, you know?

ANDY: That's really sick.

MELISSA: It is not. I don't have fantasies about him for God's sake. He just reminds me of my childhood. He would have stolen my little heart, probably broken it. And I would have thought it was the end of the world. Funny how catastrophic things seemed when we were young. I don't know. He kind of likes me and I'm flattered. That's all.

ANDY: Is that why you wore the dress? To impress a preteen?

MELISSA: Can a woman not wear a dress without it having to be for a man?

ANDY: Calling him a man is a little inaccurate, don't you think?

MELISSA: Well, he's the most interesting and honest man I've come across in the last couple years.

ANDY: That's not fair, Mel.

MELISSA: God, Andy, I didn't mean you. Don't take that personally.

ANDY: How am I supposed to take it?

MELISSA: I don't know.

ANDY: I never lied to you.

MELISSA: No, you didn't. You just quit talking altogether.

ANDY: I didn't know what to say.

MELISSA: I know. I just wish I hadn't heard about the wedding from Marc. It would have been nice to have heard it from you.

ANDY: I feel shitty about that.

MELISSA: Ah, don't.

ANDY: I do though. The least I could have done was talk to you.

MELISSA: You could've invited me to the wedding.

ANDY: I didn't think that would be appropriate, considering the circumstances.

MELISSA: I suppose not.

ANDY: I miss you, though.

MELISSA: Do you now?

ANDY: Yeah. I mean, I was crazy about you. You're one of the most beautiful people I've ever known.

MELISSA: But you married Amanda.

ANDY: Yeah, yeah I did.

MELISSA: Well, she's great.

ANDY: Yes she is. But so are you.

MELISSA: So is Jason, but I don't expect I'll marry him. Not unless I come across him in ten or fifteen years, and still think he's great.

ANDY: Hey, you never know.

MELISSA: You're a shit.

ANDY: Ooooh, ouch. That hurt.

MELISSA: Amanda's a lucky girl.

ANDY: Thank you. *(Pause.)* You want to go get some cheesecake or something?

MELISSA: I better not. I gotta get up early. I need all my energy to keep up with those kids.

ANDY: Yeah, and you'll want to look your best.

MELISSA: I always want to look my best.

ANDY: You always do. *(He goes to kiss her, she backs away.)*

ANDY: Shit, Mel, I'm sorry.

MELISSA: That's alright.

ANDY: No, it's not. That wasn't fair.

MELISSA: Really, it's alright.

ANDY: *(Pause.)* That streetlight is irritating as shit. It's distracting.

MELISSA: I used to think so. I don't know, though. He's just unique, you know? All these other streetlights are doing what is expected of them, what they're programmed to do, but he's just doing his own thing. I kind of admire his individuality.

ANDY: You're a nut, you know that?

MELISSA: I can't deny that.

ANDY: Well, I better get going. I have to stop by the store and pick up some coffee. We're out.

MELISSA: Yeah, you better. You're a bear in the morning without your coffee.

ANDY: Maybe next week we could grab dinner.

MELISSA: Maybe. You know, last weekend I went out with some friends to that new jazz club for a few drinks. We had been there a couple of hours and I noticed that I was the only single person at the table. I wasn't even really a part of the conversation. I have no significant other to gripe about. I, of course, started thinking about you. Later that night, I found myself sitting in my porch swing with my headphones on, still thinking about you. It was just me, the music, and that damn streetlight. I kept hoping I would see your car, that you would stop by. The next thing I knew, the porch swing was hanging by one chain, and I was on the ground. I felt completely ridiculous. It was at that point that I knew you had really married Amanda, that you were never coming back. Apparently, the swing knew it all along. It was fed up with me sitting there, feeling sorry for myself and feeling alone, and if all I was gonna do was think about you, then it wouldn't have me. I will always miss you, but I am going to have to learn to live with that, because I cannot live with you. You can't just come over and hang out on my porch, you have to come in or go away. You can't come in and I know that. I think you do too. That only leaves one option.

ANDY: Mel, for what it's worth…

MELISSA: Which is not much…

ANDY: Yeah, I know.

MELISSA: So, I'll see ya.

ANDY: Yeah. Okay. I'll see ya. Oh, and good luck with Jason. Let me know, I could maybe put in a good word for you.

MELISSA: Get out of here.

ANDY: Yeah. I will. I am.

(They look at each other for a moment. Andy exits.)

MELISSA: Okay.

END OF PLAY

The Divine Fallacy
by Tina Howe

CHARACTERS

VICTOR HUGO: A photographer, late thirties.
DOROTHY KISS: A writer, mid-twenties.

SETTING

Victor's studio in downtown Manhattan. It's a freezing day in late February.

The Divine Fallacy

Victor's studio in downtown Manhattan. It looks like a surreal garden blooming with white umbrellas and reflective silver screens. As the lights rise we hear the joyful bass-soprano duet, "Mit unser Macht ist nichts getan," from Bach's chorale, Ein feste Burg ist unser Gott, BWV 80. *It's a freezing day in late February. Victor, dressed in black, has been waiting for Dorothy for over an hour. There's a tentative knock at his door.*

VICTOR: Finally! *(Rushing to answer it.)* Dorothy Kiss?
　　(Dorothy steps in, glasses fogged over and very out of breath. She's a mousy woman dressed in layers of mismatched clothes. An enormous coat covers a bulky sweater which covers a gauzy white dress. A tangle of woolen scarves is wrapped around her neck.)
DOROTHY: *(Rooted to the spot.)* Victor Hugo?
VICTOR: At last.
DOROTHY: I'm sorry, I'm sorry, I got lost.
VICTOR: Come in, come in.
DOROTHY: I reversed the numbers of your address.
VICTOR: We don't have much time.
DOROTHY: *(With a shrill laugh.)* I went to 22 West 17th instead of 17 West 22nd!
VICTOR: I have to leave for Paris in an hour.
DOROTHY: The minute I got there, I knew something was wrong.
VICTOR: *(Looking at his watch.)* No, make that forty-five minutes.
DOROTHY: There were all these naked people milling around. *(Pause.)* With pigeons.
VICTOR: The spring collections open tomorrow.
DOROTHY: They were so beautiful.
VICTOR: It's going to be a mad house… Come in, please…
　　(He strides back into the studio and starts setting up his equipment.)
DOROTHY: I didn't realize they came in so many colors.

DOROTHY:	VICTOR:
Red, green, yellow, purple…	A tidal wave of photographers

I think they'd been dyed. and fashion editors is descending from all over the world.

(Pause.)

VICTOR: I swore last year would be my last, but a man's got to make a living, right? (Turning to look for her.) Hey, where did you go?
(Dorothy waves at him from the door.)

VICTOR: Miss Kiss...we've got to hurry if you want me to do this.
(Dorothy makes a strangled sound.)

VICTOR: (Guiding her into the room.) Come in, come in... I won't bite.

DOROTHY: (With a shrill laugh.) My glasses are fogged over! I can't see a thing!
(She takes them off and wipes them with the end of one of her scarves.)

VICTOR: Here, let me help you off with your coat.
(They go through a lurching dance as he tries to unwrap all her scarves, making her spin like a top.)

VICTOR: DOROTHY:
Hold still...easy does it...atta girl...   Whoops, I was just...sorry, sorry,
                                            sorry, sorry, sorry, sorry, sorry...

(He finally succeeds. They look at each other and smile, breathing heavily.)

VICTOR: So you're Daphne's sister?!

DOROTHY: Dorothy Kiss, the writer...
(Victor struggles to see the resemblance.)

DOROTHY: I know. It's a shocker.

VICTOR: No, no...

DOROTHY: She's the top fashion model in the country, and here I am...Miss Muskrat!

VICTOR: The more I look at you, the more I see the resemblance.

DOROTHY: You don't have to do that.

VICTOR: No really. There's something about your forehead...

DOROTHY: I take after my father. The rodent side of the family... Small, nondescript, close to the ground... (She makes disturbing rodent faces and sounds.)

VICTOR: You're funny.

DOROTHY: I try.
(Silence.)

VICTOR: So...

DOROTHY: (Grabbing her coat and lurching towards the door.) Goodbye, nice meeting you.

VICTOR: (Barring her way.) Hey, hey, just a minute...

DOROTHY: I can let myself out.

VICTOR: Daphne said you were coming out with a new novel and needed a photograph for the back cover.

DOROTHY: Another time…

VICTOR: It sounded wild.

DOROTHY: Oh God, oh God…

VICTOR: Something about a woman whose head keeps falling off.

DOROTHY: This was *her* idea, not mine! I hate having my picture taken! *(Struggling to get past him.)* I hate it, hate it, hate it, hate it, hate it, hate it, hate it, hate it…

VICTOR: *(Grabbing her arm.)* She told me you might react like this.

DOROTHY: *Hate it, hate it, hate it, hate it!*

VICTOR: Dorothy, Dorothy…

(Dorothy desperately tries to escape. Victor grabs her in his arms as she continues to fight him, kicking her legs. He finally plunks her down in a chair. They breathe heavily. A silence.)

DOROTHY: Why can't you set up your camera in my brain? Bore a hole in my skull and let 'er rip. *(She makes lurid sound effects.)* There's no plainness here, but heaving oceans ringed with pearls and ancient cities rising in the mist… Grab your tripod and activate your zoom, wonders are at hand… Holy men calling the faithful to prayer as women shed their clothes at the river's edge… *Click!* Jeweled elephants drink beside them, their trunks shattering the surface like breaking glass. *Click!* Their reflections shiver and merge, woman and elephant becoming one… Slender arms dissolving into rippling tusks, loosened hair spreading into shuddering flanks… *Click, click, click!* Now you see them, now you don't… A breast, a tail, a jeweled eye… *Click!* Macaws scream overhead *(Sound effect.)*, or is it the laughter of the women as they drift further and further from the shore, their shouts becoming hoarse and strange… *(Sound effect.) Click!* *(Tapping her temple.)* Aim your camera here, Mr. Hugo. *This* is where beauty lies… Mysterious, inchoate, and out of sight!

(Silence as Victor stares at her.)

DOROTHY: *(Suddenly depressed.)* I don't know about you, but I could use a drink.

VICTOR: *(As if in a dream.)* Right, right…

DOROTHY: VICTOR?! *(Pause.)* I'd like a drink, if you don't mind!

VICTOR: Coming right up. What's your poison?

DOROTHY: Vodka, neat.

VICTOR: You got it! *(He lurches to a cabinet and fetches a bottle of vodka and a glass.)*

DOROTHY: That's alright, I don't need a glass. *(She grabs the bottle and drinks an enormous amount.)* Thanks, I needed that!

VICTOR: Holy shit!

DOROTHY: *(Wiping her mouth.)* Where are my manners? I forgot about you. *(Passing him the bottle.)* Sorry, sorry…

VICTOR: *(Pours a small amount in a glass and tips it towards her.)* Cheers! *(She raises an imaginary glass.)*

DOROTHY: Could I ask you a personal question?

VICTOR: Shoot.

DOROTHY: Are you really related to Victor Hugo?

VICTOR: Strange but true.

DOROTHY: Really, really?

VICTOR: *Really!* He was my great great grandfather! *(Bowing.) A votre service.*

DOROTHY: He's my favorite writer! He's all I read… Over and over and over again! I can't believe I'm standing in the same room with you! *(She suddenly grabs one of his cameras and starts taking pictures of him.)*

VICTOR: Hey, what are you doing? That's a two-thousand-dollar camera you're using! *(He lunges for it. She runs from him, snapping his picture.)*

DOROTHY: A direct descendant of Victor Hugo…

VICTOR: *(Chasing her.)* Put that down!

DOROTHY: *(Snapping him at crazy angles.)* No one will believe me!

VICTOR: Give it here! *(Finally catching her.)* I SAID: GIVE ME THAT CAMERA! *(They struggle. A torrent of blood gushes from her hand.)*

DOROTHY: Ow! Ow!

VICTOR: *(Frozen to the spot.)* Miss Kiss…Miss Kiss…Oh my God, my God… *(Dorothy gulps for air.)*

VICTOR: What did I do? *(Her breathing slowly returns to normal.)*

VICTOR: Are you alright?

DOROTHY: *(Weakly.)* A tourniquet… I need a tourniquet.

VICTOR: On the double! *(He races around looking for one.)*

DOROTHY: Wait, my sock… *(She kicks off one of her boots and removes a white sock.)*

VICTOR: *(Running to her side.)* Here, let me help.

DOROTHY: No, I can do it. *(She expertly ties it to stop the flow of blood.)*
VICTOR: How are you feeling?
DOROTHY: Better thanks.
VICTOR: I'm so sorry.
DOROTHY: It's not your fault.
VICTOR: I didn't mean to hurt you.
DOROTHY: I have a stigmata.
VICTOR: *What?*
DOROTHY: I said I have a stigmata. It bleeds when I get wrought up.
VICTOR: *You have a stigmata?*
DOROTHY: Several, actually.
VICTOR: Jesus Christ!
DOROTHY: Jesus Christ, indeed.
VICTOR: A *stigmata?* In *my* studio?
 (Silence.)
DOROTHY: I'm afraid you're going to miss your plane to Paris. I'm sorry. *(A silence. She hands him his camera.)* Well, I guess you may as well take my picture.
VICTOR: Right, right...your picture.
 (She removes her glasses and bulky sweater and looks eerily beautiful in her white gauzy dress.)
DOROTHY: I'm as ready as I'm ever going to be.
 (Victor is stunned, unable to move.)
DOROTHY: Yoo hoo... Mr. Hugo?
VICTOR: You're so beautiful!
DOROTHY: *(Lowering her eyes.)* Please!
VICTOR: You look so sad... Like an early Christian martyr.
 (A great light starts to emanate from her. Victor races to get his camera and begins taking her picture.)
VICTOR: *(Breaking down.)* I can't...I can't...I just...can't.
DOROTHY: Victor, Victor, it's alright... We all have something... You have your eye, Daphne has her beauty and I have this. It's OK. It makes me who I am.
 (Victor struggles to control himself.)
DOROTHY: Listen to me... Listen... When the Navahos weave a blanket, they leave in a hole to let the soul out—the flaw, the fallacy—call it what you will. It's part of the design, the most important part—faith, surrender, a mysterious tendency to bleed...

VICTOR: I'm so ashamed.

DOROTHY: You did your job. You took my picture.

VICTOR: But I didn't see you.

DOROTHY: Shh, shh…

VICTOR: I was blind.

DOROTHY: Shhhhhh…

VICTOR: *(Breaking down again.)* Blind, blind, blind…

> *(Dorothy rises and places her hands over his eyes, and then raises them in a gesture of benediction.)*

DOROTHY: There, there, it's alright. It's over.

> *(The lights blaze around them and then fade as the closing measures of Bach's duet swell.)*

END OF PLAY

Carnality
by Mark Loewenstern

CHARACTERS

MICHELLE: twenty-five to thirty-five, focused, perceptive, and a little manic.

BEN: twenty-five to thirty-five, quiet, sensual, and annoyingly introverted.

Carnality

At rise: Ben's place. There are a chair and a table. On the chair is a stuffed mouse or rabbit doll. On the table are a bottle of cooking oil, a twelve-ounce piece of raw steak, a hot plate that is plugged in and already hot, a skillet on top of the hot plate, a fork, a steak knife, and whatever sauces or vegetables Ben likes with his steak. Michelle is still wearing her coat. Ben and Michelle stand hugging.

MICHELLE: Okay. *(They hug a moment longer.)* Oookay. *(A moment longer, and then Michelle pulls away.)* So. How've you been?

BEN: Good.

MICHELLE: I could have come by later. I didn't know you were eating.

BEN: I'm not eating. I'm cooking. *(Ben pours the oil into the skillet. He spends the rest of the play frying the steak. He turns it frequently, and cuts it once or twice to check its progress.)*

MICHELLE: Why are you...?

BEN: The stove is out.

MICHELLE: Oh.

BEN: Gas guy is coming Monday. So I'm making do.

MICHELLE: If you find you need a new one, go see my cousin Frank.

BEN: Really? I mean, I thought after the split, I shouldn't expect any favors.

MICHELLE: Nah, it's fine. So where's the rodent? *(Ben points to the doll. Michelle picks it up.)* She said she couldn't get to sleep without it.

BEN: Then why does she keep forgetting it everywhere?

MICHELLE: You know, we still have to discuss where she's going to school.

BEN: All right.

MICHELLE: So?

BEN: I mean, it's whatever you want, Michelle.

MICHELLE: Well, fine. I want her to go to St. Bart's. Okay? *(Beat.)* It's not okay.

BEN: It's not my first choice. I figured you'd know that. I mean, Catholic school...that brings up the whole religion issue.

MICHELLE: Yes it does.

BEN: Yes it does.

MICHELLE: Well, then it's not whatever I want, Ben. Okay? And at some point you're going to have to hash it out with me. You always do this. And it's really annoying.

BEN: What's annoying?

MICHELLE: …Forget it.

BEN: So I hear you're seeing someone.

MICHELLE: Who told you that?

BEN: Um. I don't know.

MICHELLE: You don't know?

BEN: I just brought it up because I thought it was good news.

MICHELLE: Sure, I've been on some dates.

BEN: Well, I know *that*.

MICHELLE: But I'm not seeing anyone. Who said this?

BEN: Someone said they saw you at a restaurant with a guy, and it looked like you two were clicking.

MICHELLE: Oh, jeez. Yes, yes. I remember. I ran into your friend at the sushi place. Whatshisname. Ben, what's his name?

BEN: …Zack.

MICHELLE: Zack! Thank you. I ran into Zack when I was on a date. But I wasn't seeing the guy.

BEN: All right.

MICHELLE: It was a date.

BEN: Second date? Third date?

MICHELLE: …First date.

BEN: *(Innocently.)* Oh, is it another first date?

MICHELLE: Ben. Can we drop this?

BEN: Sure. You look good, Michelle.

MICHELLE: So what are we doing about school? Because we're really running out of time on this.

BEN: I don't know.

MICHELLE: You don't know. Have you looked into other places that you'd like to send her to?

BEN: No.

MICHELLE: That's great. Do you even know how to go about doing that?

BEN and MICHELLE: No.

MICHELLE: Jesus, Ben. Why do I have to think for both of us? Still. Why do I still have to do that? *(Beat.)* There's a website with information on all the kindergartens in the city. I'll e-mail you the address.

BEN: All right.

MICHELLE: And please look at it tomorrow. And call me about it. Okay?

BEN: I will.

MICHELLE: Fine. I'm going.

BEN: All right. Bye. *(Ben reaches forward to hug her. Michelle pulls back.)*

MICHELLE: Uh. Could we not do that anymore?

BEN: Not hug?

MICHELLE: Yeah. Is that okay?

BEN: Sure. Can I ask why?

MICHELLE: I just can't.

BEN: Did I do something?

MICHELLE: I don't know.

BEN: What did I do?

MICHELLE: I just think that this whole amicable divorce thing is not working for me anymore.

BEN: All right. It was your idea.

MICHELLE: I know.

BEN: You said it'd be better for Sophie if we tried to stay friends.

MICHELLE: Well, I was wrong.

BEN: All right. So I shouldn't talk to Frank about the stove?

MICHELLE: No, you can talk to Frank about the stove, Ben. You just can't talk to me about my love life. And I can't talk to you about yours. And we should spend more time arguing about where Sophie is going to kindergarten. And basically, I just need to hate you more, okay?

BEN: Not really.

MICHELLE: Do you understand that we are not getting back together?

BEN: That's not what we're talking about.

MICHELLE: Well, guess what? It is. We are not getting back together. I don't want you back. Ever. Because you drive me nuts. And I say that without the teeniest bit of affection. You drive me absolutely coo-coo-for-Cocoa-Puffs. And I can't live with you.

BEN: I know that.

MICHELLE: Okay.

BEN: So that means you have to hate me?

MICHELLE: Yeah. Pretty much.

BEN: Why?

MICHELLE: Because otherwise I get confused.

BEN: Confused.

MICHELLE: Yes. Like this.

BEN: Like what?

MICHELLE: Like *this*. When we're together. Okay?

BEN: All right.

MICHELLE: Understand?

BEN: ...No.

MICHELLE: When we hug, it confuses me.

BEN: All right. How?

MICHELLE: I respond to you.

BEN: So?

MICHELLE: My *body* responds to you.

BEN: ...Oh.

MICHELLE: And don't take this the wrong way, but it's not like I don't meet men who are sexier than you. I do. But you're... I don't know. You're familiar. I know you. My body knows you. Isn't that the word they use in the Bible? Knowing? Adam knew Eve and David knew Bathsheba and so on and so on.

BEN: Yes. Carnal knowledge.

MICHELLE: Well, it's a good word for it. Because when you hug me, or touch me, or even when we're just alone in a room, I'll think, "This is the man I remember. This is the one I used to fall asleep next to." And it hardly even matters that at the same time I'll be thinking, "This is also the one who drives me up a tree." So it sucks, Ben. Because I don't want you to be the man I feel this way about. I want it to be someone I can live with. And I know that some day I'm going to find him...

BEN: Right.

MICHELLE: ...but I haven't yet, and it's been a while. It's been too long. And I just don't trust myself around you anymore. It feels too good when you hold me.

BEN: All right.

MICHELLE: Understand now?

BEN: Yeah.

MICHELLE: Okay.

BEN: But I mean, I feel the same way, Michelle.

MICHELLE: What way?

BEN: When you hold me, I respond too.

MICHELLE: Well, of course you do. You're a man.

BEN: So?

MICHELLE: So whatever. So goodbye.

BEN: I daydream about you. *(Beat.)* And these are not like your regular, run-of-the-mill daydreams. They're elaborate. I know all the details. No, I do. Even when I'm making it up. I know the place: what apartment we're living in, what hotel we're staying at, what beach we're lying on. I know the time: if we're up early, or up late, or if it's some rainy afternoon. I know what clothes you're wearing: which black dress, which pair of blue jeans. I know what you have on underneath them.

MICHELLE: Ben…

BEN: I know how your hair is: up or down, curled, wet.

MICHELLE: Why are you telling me this?

BEN: Why not, honey? I'm not over you either. *(Beat.)* I know what you smell like. Which perfume, which shampoo. I could tell you the shade of lipstick and nail polish. I know every last part of you that I touch: all the obvious places, and all the secret ones.

MICHELLE: Which are the secret ones?

BEN: The ones I know you like.

MICHELLE: Um…

BEN: Like your back.

MICHELLE: My back?

BEN: Just under the shoulder blades, where you like to be kissed.

MICHELLE: Oh. Right.

BEN: And behind your knee, but only if I wet my finger first. Otherwise it tickles too much. Right?

MICHELLE: Yeah.

BEN: And…the tender part of your breast.

MICHELLE: The *what?*

BEN: The tender—

MICHELLE: Which is the tender part?!

BEN: *(Demonstrating on his own body.)* The outside. Here. Where it faces your arm.

MICHELLE: Ben…this isn't fair.

BEN: No. It's not. But I don't want it to stop, either, you know? *(Beat.)*

MICHELLE: Shit. *(She sits down in the chair and starts shrugging off her coat. Ben takes a few steps toward her.)* Hey. Where are you going?

BEN: Who me?

MICHELLE: You.

BEN: Nowhere.

MICHELLE: Well then, go back.

BEN: Go back?

MICHELLE: Go back over there. Not yet. Okay?

BEN: All right. *(Ben returns to the table.)*

MICHELLE: Just a little bit longer. I like watching you cook. *(She watches him. He watches her watching him. Two small mischievous smiles. Ben looks down. It's time to turn the steak again. Slow fade as he does so.)*

END OF PLAY

Precipice
by William Mastrosimone

CHARACTERS

SHE

HE

TIME

An hour before dark in July.

PLACE

Mount Rainier, Washington.

SET

A precipice (perhaps the edge of the stage). A small fir tree.

Precipice

Sound of wind. Lights up with diffuse gray light. Enter young woman. She removes her backpack. Enter young man.

SHE: Ready?

HE: This is the place?

SHE: Absolutely. I remember this tree.

HE: There's only fifty trillion trees around us, and you remember this particular tree.

SHE: The way it grows out of the rock. Unless you want to, I'll jump first.

HE: I've seen a hundred trees growing out of rock.

SHE: No. I remember this curve in the lower trunk, how the north wind must've forced the tree to grow crooked.

HE: Heliotropism. Grows towards the southern exposure.

SHE: That's east.

HE: Can't be east. There's the last light. That's west. So that way has to be south.
(She looks at compass.)

SHE: Hmmm. You're right. I've gotten turned around by the terrain.

HE: And I'm not an outdoor guy.

SHE: Then you toss the packs over to me. Ready?

HE: Almost. *(He takes off one of his boots.)*

SHE: Pebble?

HE: Boots. Too big. Told you I should've gotten a size smaller.

SHE: Not with hiking socks. Are those cotton?

HE: Yeah.

SHE: What happened to the wool socks?

HE: Wool irritates my skin. Makes my feet sweat.

SHE: Wool breathes moisture away. Cotton holds it. "Cold feet—you're beat."

HE: You're just full of those mountaineer sayings.

SHE: Ready?

HE: You're sure this is where we jumped over this morning?

SHE: Positive.

HE: Wish I could see the ledge over there.

SHE: Been hiking this trail half my life. You could get a cold northwester on a July day, that fog pours off the snow like smoke. *(Consults watch-thermometer.)* Since we stopped here it dropped another six degrees. We really have to move.

HE: Let's go.

SHE: You okay about it?

HE: I wish I felt better about it.

SHE: You're not a hundred percent?

HE: I know I can jump the five feet across. Did it this morning.

SHE: But?

HE: It's just—

SHE: Damn fog—

HE: Yeah. I wish I could see the other side.

SHE: *(Picks up a small stone.)* Scientific method. Observe. I'm going to throw a stone. *(Tosses stone across the precipice. We hear it hit rock.)* Q.E.D. Okay?

HE: No.

SHE: Didn't you hear the stone hit the ledge over there?

HE: I heard the stone hit stone. Whether it's the ledge we jumped from I have no idea. And neither do you.

SHE: What else could it be?

HE: I don't know, and neither do you.

(She picks up another stone.)

SHE: Okay, listen to this stone.

HE: Hey, you could throw stones over all day long but no way I'm jumping where I can't see.

SHE: For one thing, we don't have all day. If we don't jump now, we're gonna get caught in a blizzard.

HE: I still don't think this is where we jumped over. Why'd you pick *this* day? Didn't you listen to a weather report?

SHE: Look, Mount Rainier—

HE: I mean, a meteorologist can see a storm coming.

SHE: Rainier makes its own weather. It's unpredictable. Even after we jump we still have six or seven thousand feet to descend. I really think we need to move on.

HE: Need a break. *(He opens his pack, takes out potato chips.)*

SHE: We need to keep ahead of the storm.

HE: My sugar's low.

SHE: Minutes are gonna count. We can eat later.

HE: I feel weak. I need some energy to jump.

SHE: This might do you better. Trail mix. *(She offers him a plastic bag out of her pack.)*

HE: I'll stay with the potato chips.

SHE: All that salt's only gonna make you thirsty. *(He takes a drink from his canteen, offers it to her; She rejects it.)* Which makes you urinate more, which rids you of more electrolytes, which makes you tired.

HE: Excuse me for being human.

SHE: You must've stopped a half a dozen times—

HE: So who's counting?

SHE: Takes a toll, that's all I'm saying. That's why you're tired. All you eat's junk. It's times like these when the discipline pays off.

HE: Times like these I don't need a lecture on health.

SHE: Sorry.

HE: No big deal.

SHE: Actually—never mind.

HE: What?

SHE: Wanna take a few practice starts and sort of sneak up on it? Let's stretch. C'mon.

HE: My legs are fine. It's my brain.

SHE: If I jumped, would that convince you?

HE: It would convince me you're out of your mind.

SHE: What if I jumped and landed safely?

HE: And what if you're wrong?

SHE: How can I be wrong? Nobody moved the mountain.

HE: You're so cocksure. You wouldn't even consider the possibility you might be mistaken?

SHE: We did it this morning, we can do it again.

HE: And what if you fall to your death?

SHE: C'mon.

HE: Or worse.

SHE: What could be worse?

HE: You fall down that chasm with a broken back, you're in terrible pain, and I'm up here unable to help.

SHE: I'm prepared for that.

HE: Who could possibly be prepared for that?

SHE: I know anything can happen up here. Rock slide. Avalanche. Run across a grizzly and her cubs. Just stumble and fall. Worse can happen in Seattle.

HE: Would you dash across the street if you were blind?

SHE: It's not the same thing.

HE: You're right. A blind person knows there's the other side of the street. Knows drivers have car brakes.

SHE: Your fear is talking.

HE: Where I come from they call it smarts. This is a helluva first date.

SHE: After I jump, toss the packs over, and toss 'em high. Better to overshoot. Just note where I jump. *(Lays a stone on the ledge.)* Let this be your marker. Jump off that marker. Give yourself enough running space. Measure it out a few times. And remember, jump high. Only bad thing is you sorta come in for a crash landing because you can't see how to break your fall. Okay? *(She stands back to give herself running room.)*

HE: Unbelievable.

SHE: What?

HE: You're really gonna run and leap into the fog not knowing what's over there?

SHE: I know what's over there.

HE: You don't know. You believe. You hope. You wish. You pray. You don't know the difference between what you know and what you hope.

SHE: You heard the stone land on that ledge.

HE: Stone hit stone. Period. That's a typical you-ism. You hope a ledge is there, therefore, a ledge's over there. No! There's rock over there. It may be flat. Or it may be round. It may be vertical. It may be horizontal. It's not a fact because you said it. It's only a fact when I can see it.

SHE: So what do you suggest we do?

HE: I don't know. Find a fallen tree. Make a bridge.

SHE: Brilliant. Trust a tree that's been down for years, full of termites.

HE: This is nuts.

SHE: Nuts will be when that blizzard catches up to us. Nuts is wasting precious time.

HE: We jumped over here to take a shortcut. Why don't we backtrack and go the long way?

SHE: Can't. We'd have to walk two hours right into the storm.

HE: Then we wait out the storm.

SHE: In shorts and t-shirts? A storm like this can have arctic winds up to seventy-five miles per. That's hurricane speed. That's hypothermia. It could dump two, three, four feet of snow on us in six hours. Wet snow. And that's death. We won't survive it. This mountain kills disrespectors. We stay, we die. Horribly.

HE: If you knew there could be blizzards in July up here, why'd you come unprepared?

SHE: I goofed.

HE: Oh—you mean you can be wrong sometimes?

SHE: I'm not wrong about the ledge.

HE: You thought east was south—and you're gonna jump?

SHE: Now if you would please get out of my way, I'm gonna prove it to you.

HE: You're so certain.

SHE: Move, please.

HE: You're so absolute about what you can't see.

SHE: I know in my heart it's there.

HE: You don't know anything.

SHE: Move.

HE: This is a helluva first date.

SHE: Also the last.

HE: No question about it.

SHE: You're just a cat up a tree. This morning you leaped across laughing. But now your body quits on you, so you start manufacturing reasons not to jump back. You're tired. You're spent. And fear's got the best of you.

HE: *(Imitating her.)* "Hey, wanna take a shortcut?" What was I thinking when I said yes?

SHE: Yeah, what were you thinking?

HE: Never scored on a mountain top before. Thought you wouldn't want to keep seeing a guy who wasn't as crazy as you. So I jumped. Of my own free will. You didn't make me. All the things we said to one another. I thought if I didn't go into your world, and take all the chances, we'd never be close. I didn't know it would kill me. Just go.

SHE: I can't just go. I'm responsible for getting you on this side. Let's hold hands and jump together. C'mon.

HE: What?

SHE: We throw the packs over, stand way, way back, take a running leap across. We can do it.

HE: You're truly out of your mind.

SHE: You may be afraid of that leap now, but when those winds hit you, when you feel your core heat dropping and start hallucinating and all you want to do is sleep, a part of you may come to your senses, but it'll be too late. You'll be even weaker, even more afraid.

HE: Let's make a shelter.

SHE: Out of what?

HE: Trees.

SHE: What trees?

HE: Branches. Anything.

SHE: You think it's easy?

HE: We'll figure it out.

SHE: Lifetime woodsmen would be hard-pressed.

HE: You go on. When you get back, tell 'em where I am.

SHE: I worked Search and Rescue. They don't go out in bad storms. They jeopardize lives for lives to a point. This storm is that point. To get you out of here, they need a six-man foot and dog unit. They have to carry a ten-foot ladder and litter up six thousand feet. The snow will be too deep. They'll wait it out. The helicopter won't fly in a blizzard. Won't fly in winds over forty miles per hour. Maybe they'll come. Maybe they won't. Maybe all they need is a bodybag. Then again, there might be lots of other goofs for S&R to fetch. There's two skeletons hanging from ropes on the southeast precipice. Mountain climbers. Been hanging there for years. Two ribcages, a bit of vertebrae, swinging on the end of a rope in the wind. Nobody can get to them. Swinging in the wind. Back and forth. Untouchable.

HE: Damn.

SHE: You did it before.

HE: That was a lifetime ago.

SHE: It was eight hours ago. You did it before. You can do it again.

HE: This is definitely not the spot. When I jumped over, I scraped my knee.

SHE: So what.

HE: I looked down on rock.

SHE: I'm sorry, I can't listen to any more of this.

HE: Saw my blood on rock.

SHE: I have to save my life.

HE: There's no blood on that rock.

SHE: For what it's worth, I've heard it said that freezing's the kindest death. It's painful at first, but after threshold's reached, numbness takes over and all you'll want to do is sleep. Then you'll curl up and fade away.

HE: Who would know that?

SHE: It's a medical fact.

HE: Who came back from the dead to make it a fact?

SHE: Believe what you want to believe. I believe we're being tested.

HE: Don't get mystical on me. I need real.

SHE: I know this trail.

HE: Like east is west. You think you know a lot of things. You say things like "Mount Rainier's holy." It's a big rock, okay? "Rainier makes its own weather." If you knew anything, we'd have the right gear, wouldn't we?

SHE: I'm moving on.

HE: Wrong about south being east.

SHE: Here's my pack.

HE: Why can't you be wrong about the precipice?

SHE: You'll find a windbreaker—

HE: Answer me.

SHE: And some food. I suggest you wait as long as possible before you consume the food—

HE: Moron.

(She picks up a crumpled ball of gum-wrapper foil.)

SHE: This is the spot. You dropped this before. Your gum wrapper.

HE: I picked mine up.

(He digs in pocket for several yellow gum-wrappers with their silver foil.)

SHE: You have four wrappers but only three foils. One's missing. And this is it.

HE: The foil you found's weathered. That's been here.

SHE: Nobody comes here.

HE: We did.

SHE: Then where's the fourth foil?

HE: Probably on my car floor. Or in the ashtray. I put my body where my mouth is. Show me blood on that rock and I'll jump. Right now. Show me. Right now. I'll go first. Just show me.

SHE: I can't.

HE: No, you can't.

SHE: I can only show you by jumping.

HE: Then why don't you? *(Beat.)* Huh? *(Beat.)* Go on. Nobody's in your way.

SHE: I can't now...

HE: Spooked?

SHE: I was so sure.

HE: Guess what? You're a human being.

SHE: Don't know how this could happen to me.

HE: Damn fog.

SHE: Of all people.

HE: The terrain.

SHE: Yeah.

HE: So what should we do?

SHE: I don't know. Don't know.

(She opens her pack, puts on her windbreaker. She sits, eyes fixed on the ledge.)

HE: I'll look for some firewood.

(He starts to exit but stops. Lights begin to fade. He looks at her. She never takes her eyes off the ledge. Lights fade to black.)

END OF PLAY

Lift and Bang
Julie Marie Myatt

CHARACTERS
GRACE
BEN

TIME
Present.

PLACE
South.

SETTING
Summer heat. A back porch with a large wooden table and an old wicker rocking chair.

Lift and Bang

Grace spreads flour on a table, wiping sweat from her forehead. She wears little clothing, and her hair is tied loosely away from her face. She takes a ball of dough from a bowl on a wicker chair and rolls it in flour. She lifts and bangs the dough on the table; lifts and bangs, lifts and bangs. She looks up, down, then quickly looks up again in the same direction. She returns her eyes to the dough and lifts and bangs. Ben enters freshly dressed and smiling.

BEN: I thought it was you out here.

GRACE: Did you. *(Kneading.)*

BEN: Looks like you're working hard.

GRACE: Yeah.

BEN: You're always work—

GRACE: Smells like you just got out of the shower.

BEN: My second one today. Goddamn heat.

   (Silence.)

BEN: Looks like you could do with one.

   (Grace continues kneading.)

BEN: What are you making?

GRACE: What's it look like?

BEN: Work.

GRACE: Yeah.

BEN: Why are you out here?

GRACE: Kitchen's too hot. Air conditioning's broke.

BEN: You got someone to fix it?

GRACE: Yeah.

BEN: Soon?

GRACE: Yeah.

BEN: What kind is it?

GRACE: Kind's what?

BEN: That bread.

GRACE: Rye.

BEN: Oh. *(Wipes his forehead with his sleeve. Mumbles.)* I always liked that kind—

GRACE: How's Beth? *(Lifts and bangs.)*

BEN: A, fine. I think she's fine.

GRACE: She's due soon, isn't she?

BEN: Next month.

GRACE: Time went quickly.

BEN: I guess it did.

GRACE: Yeah.

BEN: It did.

GRACE: *(Wipes forehead.)* You must be excited.

BEN: About what?

(Grace looks at him.)

BEN: Oh, well, yeah. I guess I am.

GRACE: *(Lifts and bangs.)* You got names picked?

BEN: Beth's got some.

GRACE: How about you?

BEN: I'll let her decide. I'm not particular.

GRACE: I guess not.

BEN: *(Touching the table.)* You want some help?

GRACE: *(Kneading.)* No.

BEN: C'mon.

GRACE: You just got cleaned up.

BEN: I don't care.

GRACE: You'll have to shower again.

BEN: *(Rolling up his sleeves.)* That's all right. C'mon.

GRACE: Suit yourself. *(Motions beside her.)*
       (Ben walks closely behind her to the chair. Grace stops kneading and looks straight ahead. Ben takes a ball of dough from the bowl. Glancing at Grace, he moves slowly behind her.)

BEN: Feels sticky.

GRACE: Put it on the table. You gotta roll it in flour.

BEN: *(Moves to her side.)* Feels kinda strange, doesn't it? Like how your insides would feel or something.

GRACE: I never felt my insides.

BEN: *(Playing with dough.)* Well, if you did.

GRACE: Never thought about it.

BEN: Hell. IF you thought about it. IF this was your guts. *(Rolling a tube of dough—holding it up.)* Huh? Or IF this was your stomach. *(Makes a clump of the tube.)* Just after you ate. Or if this was your heart. *(Makes a heart shape, holds it up to her face.)*

GRACE: Your real heart don't look like that.

BEN: It might feel like this.

GRACE: Never felt it.

BEN: Don't you think it might feel all wet and gooey like this?

GRACE: I wouldn't know.

BEN: Then how do you know what it looks like?

GRACE: I've seen pictures.

BEN: Did it look like it might feel sticky like this?

GRACE: I don't know. It looked bloody.

BEN: Well, did it—

GRACE: I don't know. It was dead. Stop playing with the damn dough.

BEN: Show me how to get it like yours.

GRACE: Bang it on the table like this. *(Lifts and bangs.)* And then knead it.

BEN: What's that do?

GRACE: Helps it rise.

BEN: Oh. *(Struggling.)* It's all stuck to my fingers.

GRACE: You played with it too long. *(Kneads.)*

BEN: *(Unbuttoning his shirt.)* Goddamn heat.

GRACE: You don't have to help—

BEN: I want to. *(Takes off his shirt.)*
     (Silence.)

GRACE: *(Glancing at his chest.)* You look skinnier.

BEN: *(Looks at himself.)* Do I?

GRACE: *(Lifts and bangs.)* Beth not feeding you enough?

BEN: Suppose I don't have the appetite I used to.

GRACE: *(Kneading.)* You look good.

BEN: So do you—

GRACE: I didn't mean it like that. I mean you look healthy. You look better skinny.

BEN: Oh. Thanks. *(Lifts and bangs.)* Is this right?

GRACE: You need more flour. *(Leans over and pours some from a bag.)*

BEN: Did you lose it?

GRACE: What?

BEN: The necklace.

GRACE: No.

BEN: What'd you do with it?

GRACE: Nothing.

BEN: Your neck looks naked.

GRACE: *(Kneading.)* So?

BEN: So it's strange to see nothing there.

GRACE: Then don't look.

BEN: *(Rolls his dough in flour.)* It looked pretty on you.

GRACE: Think I need to wear more reminders than I already got?

BEN: *(Lifts and bangs.)* No.

GRACE: Then shut up. *(Wipes her hair from her face.)*

BEN: *(Wipes his hands on his pants and moves behind her.)* Here. *(He brushes her hair from her face and unties it, letting it fall on her shoulders.)*
(Grace stops kneading and closes her eyes... Ben ties her hair up again and begins to touch her shoulders—)

GRACE: *(Opens her eyes.)* Thank you, Ben.

BEN: *(Moves his hands.)* It was falling in your face.

GRACE: I know. That's much better. Thanks.

BEN: You're welcome.

GRACE: Move.

BEN: Can't I stand here?

GRACE: No.

BEN: Why not?

GRACE: I don't want you to.

BEN: What if your hair falls again?

GRACE: I don't care. Please. It's too hot—

BEN: Wait. *(Blows.)* I'll blow on your neck to cool you. I'll keep—

GRACE: No...please—

BEN: *(Blows.)* It'll keep you nice and cool. Just like the ocean—

GRACE: No— *(Kneads slowly.)*

BEN: All that sand. All over us. Watching the waves come closer. Drinking tequila. Lifting you up and down into the water. Too drunk to move. Squeezing, rubbing those limes on your *(Grace touches her neck.)* belly. *(Blows.)* You tasted all sweet and sour. Salty lips.

GRACE: Ben—

BEN: *(Moves to other side of her neck—blows.)* Winter, baby. When we rode my motorcycle to the city. Smoking cigarettes on the side of the road. Playing we were drifters. That leather—

GRACE: Stop—

BEN: Outfit I bought you. Your hair all tangled.

GRACE: Ben—

BEN: *(Blows.)* Sleeping outside. You underneath me. So soft and warm. Moving. Melting. Spreading—

GRACE: *(Moves away from him.)* I said stop.

BEN: I don't want to.

GRACE: I do. *(Lifts and bangs the dough Ben started.)* I've got things to do.

BEN: Let me do that.

GRACE: You've played with it enough.

BEN: I was just learning. Let me help.

GRACE: You aren't helping.

BEN: C'mon. *(Reaches for dough.)*

GRACE: *(Moving away.)* No.

BEN: Grace—

GRACE: Beth will be wondering where you are.

BEN: I don't care.

GRACE: Go anyway.

BEN: Why?

GRACE: I'm asking you to.

BEN: Ever think of asking me to stay?

GRACE: No.

BEN: I don't love her.

GRACE: *(Kneading.)* That's too bad.

BEN: I never did.

GRACE: Well—

BEN: Never.

GRACE: You didn't have to.

BEN: I can leave her.

GRACE: Don't.

BEN: I miss you.

GRACE: Good.

BEN: I can leave her, Grace.

GRACE: *(Lifts and bangs.)* Don't bother.

BEN: I miss you.

GRACE: *(Looks at him.)* I heard you. And I say, don't bother.

BEN: Why?

GRACE: *(Kneading.)* You better get on home. Beth'll be worried.

BEN: I don't care!

GRACE: She'll be waiting for you.

BEN: I don't love her.

GRACE: *(Lifts and bangs.)* Waiting in that bedroom.

BEN: Gracie—

GRACE: *(Kneading.)* Right where you found her.

BEN: Grace—

GRACE: Right where you got her. You got her.

BEN: I never—

GRACE: *(Putting dough in pans.)* Underneath you. You got her.

BEN: I want you. *(Tries to touch her.)*

GRACE: You got yourself a little family.

BEN: I want you. *(Touches her.)*

GRACE: *(Knocks his hand away.)* Go home. *(She sits down in chair.)*

BEN: *(Picks up his shirt.)* This is my home.

GRACE: My home.

BEN: I miss you.

GRACE: MY home. MY house. MY porch. MY table. MY bread. MY chair. *(Pulls down hair.)* MY hair. MY lips. MY heart.

BEN: My—

GRACE: Nothing. Go home.

BEN: *(Puts on shirt—mumbles.)* My love—

GRACE: She's waiting. *(Rubs her neck.)*

    (Lights dim.)

END OF PLAY

What I Came For
by Alice O'Neill

CHARACTERS
AMY

JOHN

What I Came For

At rise: Amy sits at the bar, speaks to John, the Irish bartender. Her eyes are on the door. She's tipsy.

AMY: I'm so glad *they're* gone. Soap people. I mean, did you pick up on that? Well, when you're in a room where half the guys are named Jeremy and there's more hair gel per capita then anywhere in Italy. That's how you know you're in a room full of soap people. What's so hard about memorizing that drivel? They're really good at furrowing their brows.

Not that I have anything against soap operas. Actually, I do have something against soap operas. They're just not what they used to be, know what I mean? It used to be like, "Oh, Godfrey, I'm in love with Chad, even though he's on trial for murder!" But now the soaps are all, "Oh, Clay, Monica's having a crack baby! Let's all turn out to show her how much we support her and love her for it!"

JOHN: Last call.

AMY: Already? Well. I'll have another *pint.* Another *pint,* please. This place is really authentic. Why do they call it The Great Eastern Rock?

JOHN: Don't know.

AMY: Where I live, all the Irish bars are called things like, Michael Patrick O'Shea McCleery's Place. They string a bunch of Irish-sounding names together and to them that spells *fun.* But this place is like the real thing. Not that I've ever been to Ireland, but if you're in Ireland, you don't have to go out of your way to let people know they're in an Irish Pub. Right? Where are your people from?

JOHN: My *people?*

AMY: Mine are from County Tyrone. That's in the North.

JOHN: I've heard of it.

AMY: Though I'm almost ashamed to say it, what with the "troubles" and all. You don't hold it against me, do you?

JOHN: Very much so.

AMY: I'm the one who knew about this place. I'm the one who suggested it to Kara. Then she was all, oh, there's this really gritty little Irish Pub over in Montauk! Let's go, everybody! As if it was her discovery. She was the one everybody was toasting; did you see her? As if you could miss her, in that tacky wedding dress. I'm surprised she even made it down the aisle in that antebellum hoop skirt she was wearing. And everybody's all, "Isn't Kara the most beautiful bride you've ever seen?" And I just want to say, number one, either you've been going to a lot of weddings in Appalachia or you're blind; and two, her name isn't really Kara; it's *Carol.* Not Kara, Carol! Sometimes I think, this is something *Soap Opera Digest* might like to know. She can just get over herself. I mean, so what if she bought her own fax machine? That doesn't make her half the mature person she thinks she is. And, not to mention that her father paid the rent the whole time we lived together. I had to hold down two jobs. She just sat at home doing I don't know what. Sending faxes. Okay and now she's on a soap and married to the perfect guy with the house in Amagansett. Another Daddy to pay the rent. I wouldn't be her for all the tea in China.

When she first moved in, Carol—I mean *Kara*—used to say we were a great team. Like Laverne and Shirley, she used to say. Like, TV's first *lesbians?* Whatever.

What's on the jukebox? *(Amy goes and checks out the jukebox.)* My Da used to play the Clancy brothers at home. Any Clancy Brothers?

JOHN: I don't think so.

AMY: Watch this. *(Amy does a few* Riverdance *steps for John.)*

I bought the videotape and taught myself. Not too bad, right? There's this guy works with me at Pottery Barn—he says he's not gay, whatever. But his sister-in-law is a Rockette and she can get free tickets to certain things at Radio City Music Hall so this guy is going to see if he can get me in to see the *Lord of the Dance* next time he comes. I'm not a real dancer, it's just something I like to do for myself, if you know what I mean. It's just mine; it's like just because I enjoy something doesn't mean I have to make money off of it, or try to make a *career* out of it. I'm pretty sure they're going to make me assistant manager after Christmas, so. *(John puts chairs on tables.)* Oh, you're closing up. Okay. So I should pay, right?

JOHN: Three fifty for that last one.

AMY: So how long have you been here?

JOHN: Eleven and a half hours.

AMY: No! How long have you been in the *States?*

JOHN: Even longer.

AMY: And do you miss Ireland?

JOHN: No.

AMY: It's just something in the blood, isn't it? I've never been to Ireland and I'm pretty far removed, but there's something about the music and the language that calls me back.

JOHN: What language? English?

AMY: No, Gaelic. Do you speak it?

JOHN: Yup.

AMY: There's something really primal about it. And what's this about? *(She does some more Riverdance steps.)* Why do they keep the arms down? I have a theory. Do you want to hear it?

JOHN: More than anything.

AMY: To me it's like the ultimate in *controlled fire.* You know? It's like, my heart and my gut want to move with wild abandon, but I can't let anyone know, because that's the Irish way. Not like the Greeks with their arms flailing everywhere, kissing all the ladies. No, I can dance all day and night and no one will ever know the passion in my heart. Because that's the Irish way. My father is like that. I mean, he's mostly German, but. Anyway.

JOHN: That's three fifty for the last one.

AMY: Oh right. Oh, *ay.* So tell me about *where you're from.*

JOHN: Why?

AMY: Because I'd like to get to know you.

JOHN: Why?

(Silence. Amy practices a few more steps.)

You're not going to finish a whole pint. Here's some coffee.

AMY: Oh, don't give me coffee. Coffee makes me crazy.

JOHN: Will you have anything else then? Time to close up.

AMY: How about. Some. I don't know what I want. Wait! Yes I do. What's that? In that heart-shaped bottle there? On the back shelf?

JOHN: What, that? Tell you the truth, no one ever orders that. Probably been on the shelf for a decade.

AMY: Looks sticky. I'm Amy. *(She holds her hand out for him to shake. He does.)*

JOHN: John.

AMY: I do know what I'd like, John. *(Long silence.)*

JOHN: Well?

AMY: Could I stick around for a while? After you close up?

JOHN: Sure. But I don't know what you'd do by yourself all night, locked inside a bar.

AMY: John! No; is there somewhere you like to go? Some other pub where you hang out after this one closes? Maybe listen to some music? Have a few drinks?

JOHN: Nope.

AMY: Oh. *(Pause.)* What do you do?

JOHN: What d'you mean?

AMY: I mean. You tend bar. And what else?

JOHN: That's what I do. I tend bar.

AMY: You can't tell me you're not a writer or something.

JOHN: Nope. Just a bartender.

AMY: But you see, I love that! A guy who just is what he is! I bet you know a million jokes, too.

JOHN: I know one or two.

AMY: Tell me a joke.

JOHN: *(Reluctantly.)* Long or short?

AMY: I don't care.

JOHN: Okay. Eh. Why is a giraffe's neck so long?

AMY: I don't know. Why is a giraffe's neck so long?

JOHN: Because its head is so far away from its body. *(Pause.)*

AMY: I don't get it.

JOHN: Well, never mind.

AMY: Oh. Oh! I do get it. I get it. That's funny.

JOHN: Not really. It's just the first thing that came to mind.

AMY: Well. I got my joke. I didn't get what I came for, but I did get a laugh.

JOHN: Good night, then.

AMY: 'Night. Thanks. *(After a bit.)* Before I go. Will you kiss me? Just once. It can be anywhere. On my face. Or my shoulder, or. Doesn't matter. Just a little…peck.

JOHN: Ah, well. That's against the rules, now.

AMY: How about a caress?

JOHN: What about that guy standin' next to you at the bar? What was his name?

AMY: Jeremy.

JOHN: Why didn't you ask him for a kiss? He looked like he was good for it.

AMY: I guess I didn't notice him. I guess because I was looking so hard at you all night. *(Pause. Amy looks for her purse under the bar.)*

AMY: Where's my…? I can't find my—

JOHN: Here.

(He puts her purse up on the bar.)

JOHN: Can't trust anyone in Montauk this time of year. Not with all those soap people running around.

AMY: Three fifty? *(Amy digs in her purse; she puts a bill down on the bar.)* Maybe I'll have another wedding to come to in Montauk sometime soon. Or maybe you'll have a reason to come to the city.

JOHN: I never do.

(She pauses for a moment, then turns away from him and starts out. She turns around.)

AMY: You know, the least you could do is, I don't know. Be *charming* when you throw me out. You're Irish! Couldn't you sing me a sad lullaby; or spin me a yarn? Couldn't you weave me a *little* Irish magic?

(John's brogue thins out now.)

JOHN: You want me to spin you a yarn? Here's one. I had a wife. I had a job at the Bank of Ireland, made lots of money. Had a house; big, ugly house in Wicklow. I stayed with it for three years, then one day I woke up with a stunning hatred for all of it. Well, I told Jeanine that I was going to visit my cousin here in Montauk. I don't have a cousin here in Montauk. But I did come and I never went back.

I don't miss Ireland. My only regret is that I have to be so goddam Irish in this goddam job. But bartending suits me. I can move around. I spend my winters in Key Largo, and my summers here. Still an alien, legally, but I make enough money to get by; I learn enough jokes to keep people happy; and I meet enough women to keep me down.

Now, that's the truth of me, and probably thousands of others like me. Just a little tip for you. Better just to steer clear.

AMY: Well. I guess you've done the honorable thing. All I wanted was a little, I don't know. Contact. But this is better than nothing. *(She starts to leave.)*

JOHN: Amy. Show me that shoulder of yours. *(After a moment, she lifts up her sleeve and bears her shoulder. He approaches her. He kisses her shoulder, then her neck, and her forehead. She throws her arms around him. He gently pushes her away.)*

JOHN: Good night.

AMY: Thanks.

(She exits. John goes behind the bar; puts on the Clancy Brothers. He whistles along as he puts chairs up on tables.)

END OF PLAY

Hiss
by Jett Parsley

CHARACTERS
JOHN
ALEX

Hiss

A dimly lit basement used as a laundry room. There are plenty of spider webs and dead insects, but the couple making out on the washing machine among the piles of dirty clothes doesn't seem to find it unappealing.

They are John and Alex, he thirty, she twenty-eight. Alex sits on the washing machine. John leans against it. They kiss passionately as they talk.

JOHN: Say you love me.

ALEX: I love you.

JOHN: Say, "I love my husband."

ALEX: I love my husband.

JOHN: Say, "I love my husband and I'll never leave him."

ALEX: I love my husband and I'll never leave him.

JOHN: *(Still kissing.)* So what got into you today? Leaving me a note in my briefcase—meet me in the laundry room. I mean, I like it, but it's a new side of you.

ALEX: You like it, huh?

JOHN: Say, "My husband really turns me on when he makes love to me in the basement on top of the washing machine."

ALEX: *(As Alex says her next line, her eyes fall on something close by, on the floor.)* My husband really...turns...me... *(She screeches and pulls away from John.)* Oh, my God! Oh my God! John—John turn around— *(She pushes John around and points to the floor.)* It's a—oh, my God! Get something! Kill it! Kill it!

JOHN: What—what do you... Oh, Alex, it's just a baby.

ALEX: Kill it right now! It's moving—it's getting away!

JOHN: It's black.

ALEX: John!

JOHN: It can't hurt you.

ALEX: It can slither up my leg and clamp onto God knows what. John, I swear! Kill it!

JOHN: It'll keep the mice down.

ALEX: I love mice. Get the hoe. *(John crosses to a wall where several garden tools lean and gets a hoe.)*

JOHN: Why do I have to do it?

ALEX: Hit it—do it—chop it in half!

JOHN: Who says it's the husband's job to kill the snake? I didn't take a vow for that.

ALEX: Quit arguing and do it.

JOHN: You do it, you want it done so bad. *(He hands Alex the hoe. She slides off the washing machine and toward the snake but steps back.)*

ALEX: I can't. I can't! I'll throw up! *(She tries to hand John the hoe.)* Look, it's headed for that hole, in the wall—John! John, if that thing ends up in our bed, you will not see *me* in that bed for a long time to come.

JOHN: Oh, all right. *(He grabs the hoe, approaches the snake, and scoops it up.)*

ALEX: Don't pick it up. Kill it! *(John swings the hoe—and the snake—to face her.)*

JOHN: It wants to say goodbye.

ALEX: Quit. *(He approaches her. She backs away.)* Stop!

JOHN: Isn't it cute? *(As the snake.)* Kissssss me, sweetie.

ALEX: No! Get it away from me!

JOHN: Ssssuch a sssssexy lady. Sssuch a lovely facccce.

ALEX: I'm going to scream!

JOHN: *(Hissing.)* Come on, beautiful, bite the apple. It tasssstes sssso good.

ALEX: *(Now backed into a corner.)* It's going to fall on me! Stop!

JOHN: No, it isn't. It's wrapped itself around the pole. See? He's looking at you. He thinks you're pretty.

ALEX: How do you know it's a he?

JOHN: You can tell by the underbelly.

ALEX: Really?

JOHN: Oh, yes. Look. *(He pushes the snake closer.)*

ALEX: No! NO! John! *(He pulls back a little, but she is still trapped.)* It's not funny. Get it away from me.

JOHN: What makes you so scared of a little snake?

ALEX: Well, you're scared of clowns!

JOHN: They aren't slimy, you know. They're smooth and cool.

ALEX: You made me take down that framed circus poster because it was giving you nightmares—big chicken!

JOHN: They just want to curl up in a quiet corner.

ALEX: Snakes can kill, but all a clown does is laugh, laugh and squirt water, and you're scared of them—your mother told me you *cried* when the clown came for your birthday—big baby—how manly is it to be afraid of a *clown? (Silence.)* Let me out of here.

JOHN: I'm not holding you.

ALEX: I can't get by.

JOHN: Do you think it's going to leap off the hoe at you? *(Pause. Alex gathers her nerve. She starts to move. John swings the hoe to block her path.)* Say you love me.

ALEX: What?

JOHN: Say you love me.

ALEX: Right now I hate you.

JOHN: Say you love me and you want to have my babies.

ALEX: Asshole.

JOHN: Say you love me and you want to have my babies and you worship the ground I walk on.

ALEX: You are going way too far.

JOHN: Say it. Or I'll put this snake around your neck.

ALEX: *(Quickly and coldly.)* I love you and I want to have your babies and I worship the ground you walk on.

JOHN: Like you mean it.

ALEX: You know, John, I never knew about this thing you have for reptiles… didn't know they turned you on. What happened? Did you go to the fair and fall in love with the snake lady?

JOHN: *(Pause.)* Yeah.

ALEX: *(Pause.)* You did?

JOHN: Actually, yeah. I was six. I went with my dad. It cost a dollar to get in.

ALEX: Tell me about her.

JOHN: She smiled at me and winked her eye.

ALEX: Was she beautiful?

JOHN: She wore a turban and played Indian music on a pipe.

ALEX: Did you talk to her?

JOHN: She said, "Stand back, boy, before you get bitten."

ALEX: *(Cautiously approaching him.)* Do you think about her?

JOHN: Sometimes.

ALEX: Would you like me to buy some rubber snakes and drape them around my breasts and hips and caress them?

JOHN: Maybe.

ALEX: Would you like me to hisssssss in your earsssssss? *(She does. John closes his eyes, turned on. Then, suddenly, Alex turns on him, shoving him and knocking him forward.)* What the *hell* is your problem—holding that snake up at me—*threatening* me—I have never seen that kind of sick, macho-man, sado crap from you before—makes me wonder what else I don't know about you—what kind of power trip are you on that you think you can treat me like that? *(John pauses, watching the snake.)*

JOHN: I don't know. I'm sorry.

ALEX: Sorry. You held a snake up to my face—you backed me into a corner—you made me… Stop looking at that thing and listen to me!

(He looks at her.)

I saw a man *die* by a snake bite once.

JOHN: You did?

ALEX: He was a snake handler. He pulled that creature out of the box and it bit him and he died.

JOHN: He died right there?

ALEX: His skin turned brown and he stopped breathing.

JOHN: You saw it?

ALEX: I saw it. I was six. I was with my mother.

JOHN: Your mother was a snake tamer?

ALEX: No, the man was.

JOHN: I had no idea.

ALEX: I don't like to talk about it.

JOHN: I can imagine. I'm sorry. I'm *really* sorry. *(Pause.)*

ALEX: I love you and I want to have your babies and I worship the ground you walk on.

JOHN: You don't have to say it.

ALEX: I just did.

JOHN: Thank you. *(He puts the hoe aside. They watch the snake slither to the floor.)*

ALEX: It's getting away.

JOHN: Do you want me to kill it?

ALEX: Oh, let it go. It's just a baby anyhow.

JOHN: Babies grow up.

ALEX: It'll keep away the mice.

JOHN: And when it eats all the mice, it'll move upstairs with us.

ALEX: We need a pet.

(They watch it disappear into the hole.)

JOHN: There. Too late now.

ALEX: Yes. Too late.

JOHN: I think it might have been a water moccasin.

ALEX: *(Pause.)* Won't make a very good pet, then.

JOHN: No.

ALEX: *(Pause.)* Did you really fall in love with a snake woman?

JOHN: No. *(Pause.)* Did you really see a man die?

ALEX: No. *(Silence.)* What just happened?

JOHN: I said I was sorry.

ALEX: Maybe that snake was an evil spirit.

JOHN: You mean like the devil?

ALEX: It came to tempt us to do evil.

JOHN: You don't even believe in God.

ALEX: Did you feel possessed?

JOHN: I didn't feel possessed.

ALEX: You weren't yourself.

JOHN: I'm always myself.

ALEX: You *weren't* yourself. *(Pause.)* You weren't yourself.

JOHN: I wasn't myself.

ALEX: You never lie.

JOHN: I never lie. *(Pause.)* It must have been an evil spirit.

ALEX: *(Pause.)* Say you love me.

JOHN: I love you.

ALEX: Say, "I love my wife."

JOHN: I love my wife.

ALEX: Say, "I love my wife and I'll never leave her."

JOHN: I love my wife and I'll never leave her.

ALEX: Good. It's good to hear you say that.

END OF PLAY

Scheherazade
by Emily Roderer

CHARACTERS

GIRL: Young. Perhaps sixteen years old.
MAN: Older.

SETTING

The early part of the twentieth century. The deck of a ship bound for North America from the Continent.

Scheherazade

The deck of a ship. Sounds of crowd, waves, and ship fade in the background. A girl, sixteen, sits in a deck chair near a man. The man is writing in a ledger.

GIRL: Are you a writer?

MAN: No.

GIRL: What are you doing?

MAN: Excuse me. Should you be talking to strangers?

GIRL: Strangers? We've been trapped on board with these people for almost two weeks. Don't you feel like you've known each and every one of them your whole life?

MAN: No.

GIRL: I do. And the rain! I've been trapped in a cabin with my aunt and my cousin for three days. I could jump overboard.

MAN: *(Continues writing.)* How dramatic.

GIRL: How do you keep from being bored?

MAN: *(Still writing.)* I work.

GIRL: *(Doesn't take the hint.)* What do you do?

MAN: I'm a banker.

GIRL: You loan people money?

MAN: Where is your aunt?

GIRL: I don't know, and I don't care. *(The man is writing again.)* I hate work.

MAN: You have to earn your keep?

GIRL: I won't have to. I'm going to marry a rich man who will take care of me.

MAN: And if you don't?

GIRL: I'll be a writer. I'm very good at stories. I've imagined a story for nearly every person on deck. Would you like to hear one?

MAN: Do I have a choice?

GIRL: See the woman over there with the funny hat and the shoes that don't fit?

MAN: Yes.

GIRL: The man to her left with the spectacle is a rich suitor. She's been tempting him the whole trip. He wants her to marry him, but she doesn't love him. She's in love with the bald man with his back to us. I've seen her pass notes to him every day. They've been lovers for years. It's so obvious, you'd think the man with the spectacle would realize, but he's a fool, so he doesn't. She marries one of these rich old fools once every...five years. Slowly, she poisons them with arsenic. When the old man croaks she sends for her bald lover and meets him on a boat, like this one, bound for Asia or Europe or maybe South America. They travel for a while together. Reaping the benefits of their merciless endeavor. Then, en route back to the United States, they find another of these bumbling idiots, like the man with the spectacle, and the wicked cycle starts all over again.

MAN: And your reasoning?

GIRL: The man with the spectacle is obviously a fool. Have you spoken to him? The woman is obviously a temptress, that's why she wears those ridiculous hats and shoes that don't fit. And the bald man is obviously her lover because he's constantly at her disposal, and she passes him notes night and day.

MAN: The bald man is a steward on this ship. He takes dinner orders. The woman is a wealthy heiress prone to wearing eccentric clothing, and the fool is a fool trying to convince her to invest in his business.

GIRL: How do you know all that?

MAN: I've had dinner with them three times.

GIRL: But isn't my story more interesting?

MAN: Yes, but only because they are so boring. And your story isn't remotely believable.

GIRL: Why not?

MAN: Because that woman isn't remotely enticing, and she'd have to be to lure money away from rich old fools.

GIRL: Enticing? Is that what you have to be?

MAN: Yes.

GIRL: And if you're not?

MAN: Well, some people have to work to earn their keep.

GIRL: Some people have to tutor their cousin in art and history and read to their aunt and get her shawl whenever she asks, and if you do something she doesn't like you apologize, and when she threatens to leave you at home on her next trip, you cry and plead, because you know being left at home is worse than being with her.

MAN: Not such a bad job, is it?

GIRL: It might be, if that's all you could do.

MAN: I have to go to work every day and count money and sign loans or not sign loans and refuse people money that they may have needed but you couldn't in good conscience let them have. And maybe they needed it because a baby was on the way or their mother was ill or they couldn't find work. Those are not easy decisions.

GIRL: You do all that?

MAN: Sometimes.

GIRL: I would like to do that. I would give them the money, if they needed it.

MAN: That's why little girls don't work in banks.

GIRL: Little girl. *(She laughs.)* That's why they study art and visit Europe with their aunts and wear gloves to parties.

MAN: Yes. *(She is silent. He is content for a moment and returns to work.)* Sometimes, I give them the money.

GIRL: I knew you did.

MAN: I make them pay it back.

GIRL: Of course, so, you can loan it to other people.

MAN: Yes, sometimes.

GIRL: I thought you had a kind face, an imaginative face. That's why I thought you were a writer. You looked as though you understood people.

MAN: Humph.

GIRL: Don't you ever imagine stories?

MAN: *(Laughs.)* My job in the bank is so much more interesting.

GIRL: Tell me a story.

MAN: I don't tell stories.

GIRL: Everyone tells stories.

MAN: Not me.

GIRL: Not ever?

MAN: No.

GIRL: Never to your son or daughter?

MAN: I don't have any children.

GIRL: Never to a niece or nephew?

MAN: I don't have any family.

GIRL: Never to a lover?

MAN: You're too young to be talking about lovers.

GIRL: No, I'm not. I have to know all about them to be a writer.

MAN: Well, then you're too young to be talking about them to me.

GIRL: Then, say something, anything.

MAN: *(He starts softly, as if he is telling a secret.)* The man and woman behind us. The two sketching. Don't look.

GIRL: Yes.

MAN: They're both world famous artists. They're married, but they're traveling together as brother and sister.

GIRL: Why?

MAN: Because they don't like to have attention drawn to themselves. They pick their subjects from ordinary people. If people knew they were famous artists, they would behave differently in front of them and none of their art would be real.

GIRL: How do you know?

MAN: I had dinner with them last night.

GIRL: And they told you all this?

MAN: I have an honest face. They thought they could trust me, and I believe they've already finished sketching me.

GIRL: Are you going to be in a painting?

MAN: Probably not. I was a useful exercise in the human form, but you never know. They could choose anyone as the subject for their next masterpiece.

GIRL: Anyone?

MAN: Anyone.

GIRL: *(She becomes self-conscious.)* How will you know, if they've used you in a painting?

MAN: You wouldn't, unless you asked.

GIRL: I'm not going to ask.

MAN: Why not? What's the harm?

GIRL: I'm not going to ask because you're not telling the truth.

MAN: I wouldn't lie.

GIRL: But you would tell a story.

MAN: I don't tell stories.

GIRL: You'd never tell me to go over and ask them if I was to be in their next painting, if they were really artists.

MAN: *(Laughs.)* Then, you learned something about telling a story.

GIRL: I knew it was a story!

MAN: But you believed me until the end.

GIRL: I didn't.

MAN: The trick is not to make the story too outrageous or ridiculous.

GIRL: How do you know about stories, if you don't tell them?

MAN: I used to tell stories.

GIRL: When?

MAN: That was a very long time ago.

GIRL: Who did you tell stories to?

MAN: A woman I used to know.

GIRL: Your wife?

MAN: No.

GIRL: Your lover?

MAN: How old are you?

GIRL: Why?

MAN: You shouldn't be discussing people's lovers. Why don't you have another try?

GIRL: Was she your mistress?

MAN: I meant why don't you tell another story?

GIRL: I know what you meant. What kind?

MAN: Tell me one that I'll believe.

GIRL: That's an awful lot of pressure.

MAN: I have faith in you.

GIRL: Who would you like me to tell a story about?

MAN: Anyone?

GIRL: Anyone on deck.

MAN: You.

GIRL: Me? *(Pause.)* I'm sixteen. I'm traveling with my aunt and my cousin, Amy. We've been abroad for the summer. My aunt took us to Europe for a bit of "culture." In my aunt's view, the trip was a miserable failure. She hired a third-rate governess to tutor us in French and take us to museums. The governess ran off with our cook.

MAN: Was he handsome?

GIRL: No, he was hideous. It wasn't romantic. She was a shrew. He had a bit of money saved. I heard them discussing it in the garden one night. That's the only reason she went off with him.

MAN: Not in the least bit exciting.

GIRL: It was sad. She didn't love him. When she left she pulled me aside and said, "Learn how to fend for yourself. Work if you have to, but it's easier if you find someone to do it for you."

MAN: Not very romantic.

GIRL: No, I'd never marry for money.

MAN: Humph.

GIRL: My aunt was forced to be chaperon. She has gout and couldn't keep up with us. Amy and I smoked our first cigarette in the gardens at Versailles. Does that shock you?

MAN: No.

GIRL: The gardens are lovely. My aunt's gout got the worst of her, and we had to stay penned in the hotel room. She tried to occupy us. Amy is eighteen, and my Aunt had wealthy suitors visit almost every day. One was an Italian nobleman. He fell in love with me. He visited every day and passed me notes. The trip ended abruptly when my aunt discovered us. She was very angry.

MAN: Because you're too young.

GIRL: No, she doesn't care about me. I have no money. She doesn't want me to marry well. She doesn't want me to marry at all. She wants me to take care of her in her old age.

MAN: You've read too many romantic novels.

GIRL: It's all true.

MAN: I believed the first part. The second part is stolen.

GIRL: He's followed me on board. He's so in love with me, he's following me back to America. He wants to elope. He's been watching us this whole time. See him. The handsome, dark man, with the wide brim hat. He thinks he's inconspicuous. Don't stare. I only decided to speak with you, because I saw him coming over, and I thought he might try to kiss me. We'd be discovered.

MAN: Now, you're being outrageous.

GIRL: It's a good story.

MAN: Oh yes. Very good for you.

GIRL: You halfway believed me.

MAN: Until it became ridiculous.

GIRL: It was more exciting than your story.

MAN: Yes, but you believed me.

GIRL: Only for a moment.

MAN: Your story would have been more believable, if the nobleman hadn't been rich.

GIRL: No?

MAN: Or maybe not a nobleman at all.

GIRL: No?

MAN: No, a commoner and your wealthy aunt threatened to cut you off if you married him.

GIRL: That's not a very happy story.

MAN: No, but maybe closer to the truth.

GIRL: But what if her money was really mine, at least some of it. And what if, I just couldn't get to it.

MAN: You'd still be in a pinch.

GIRL: But what if there was someone who could help me?

MAN: You have a fine imagination.

GIRL: And what if that person was the banker who controlled that money and all he had to do was help me just a little.

MAN: If only things were so simple.

GIRL: Did you tell the woman stories?

MAN: Oh yes.

GIRL: Were they believable?

MAN: They were hopeful.

GIRL: What happened to her?

MAN: Let's just say, she had an aunt who didn't approve.

GIRL: What if someone could have helped her?

MAN: I would have been very happy.

GIRL: And you would have paid every penny back?

MAN: Yes.

GIRL: I believe you.

END OF PLAY

Saturday Night
by Christopher Shinn

CHARACTERS

COREY

ALEX

Saturday Night

Lights rise on Corey, twenties male, and Alex, twenties female, in the living room of their apartment. They are arriving.

COREY: Well…that was good.

ALEX: It's uneven. It's inconsistent. But this was one of the better meals we've had there.

COREY: It was pretty good I thought. It's like most restaurants, you have to know what to order.

ALEX: I'm not going to get the wonton soup anymore, I'm not going to make that mistake again.

COREY: Yeah, it's really watery, isn't it?

ALEX: It's just so tepid and flavorless. *(Alex sits.)*

COREY: No, you're right, you're right. And the uh, the broccoli and beef. That sauce is just…it's like…well for one thing it's really bright *orange*, but that—*gelatinous* consistency, it's…it's…

ALEX: Disturbing.

COREY: Well, I don't know if I'd go that far. But I see what you're saying. The fortune cookies there are *great* though.

ALEX: They have that lemony bite to them.

COREY: Yeah, that's good.

ALEX: No, it *is* good. *(Pause. Corey sits, across from Alex.)*

COREY: So. What time is it?

ALEX: Six-thirty.

COREY: Six-thirty. So. Well. Where do you wanna go tonight? Have you given it any thought?

ALEX: Well, Lacey called.

COREY: Ohhh.

ALEX: She's having people over for cocktails, it's going to be small I think.

COREY: Right. *(Beat.)* She has such a smart apartment.

ALEX: What do you mean?

COREY: Just that it's decorated so simply. And tastefully. There's just—there's a real grace about it. So many apartments, they're just—I mean all our friends are starting to make a little *money* now, and—you look at their apartments, and all the furniture and everything…it looks like it's *bought*. But Lacey's apartment—has a real—a real playful, improvisational but like—like—studied, thoughtful quality to it. It has those two energies, you know, just— *(Corey makes a motion with his hands.)*

ALEX: Right. I. I think our apartment has a—grace.

COREY: Sure. Sure I mean. You know. A…vague grace.

ALEX: Vague?

COREY: Like an afterthought. Well look, I mean, we haven't, we're still trying to figure out everything we want to do, you know. With the space.

ALEX: Well…to be honest I think Lacey's kind of kind of—high strung, you know. Her apartment is very—*specific*. I think it reveals her repression.

COREY: Right, right, I see what you're saying. *(Pause.)*

ALEX: Well so maybe we'll go there but probably we won't.

COREY: Okay. *(Pause.)*

ALEX: How about a movie?

COREY: I could see a movie. What are you in the mood to see?

ALEX: I think that movie *Bridge Under Water* looks good. With the flood?

COREY: Oh, right, right, that opened today, I read a few of the reviews…

ALEX: Mm-hmm?

COREY: I keep hearing these really great things about *The Red Onion*.

ALEX: Oh, right. The farming movie…

COREY: I hear some pretty great things about it.

ALEX: It's based on that book. That I read.

COREY: Oh?

ALEX: Which was. It was a pretty pretentious book if you ask me. Very boring and grossly sentimental, unless you're interested in northeastern farming communities in the 1800s and farmers with heart murmurs—

COREY: Oh, I just remembered! My friend Tyler's in town—Tyler from…

ALEX: Tyler?

COREY: The, from school, the novelist—he's in Los Angeles now, he's here for some I dunno some research for a screenplay and he wanted to have drinks. He left a message earlier and it totally slipped my mind! I saved it on the machine. *(Corey gets up and goes to the machine.)*

ALEX: Oh, you saved it? *(Corey is at the machine.)*

COREY: It says no messages.

ALEX: I—I'm sorry. I thought you'd heard them already.

COREY: Oh. Oh well. Maybe he'll…call again.

ALEX: What's Tyler up to these days? *(Corey pours a drink.)*

COREY: Well, if you're not up to anything tonight, my friend Barbara you remember her right, and her friend Ellen, her friend, invited me out to dinner at the Wharf. *(Corey goes and sits.)*

ALEX: Oh. Well Michelle and Gregory, actually I guess they have this documentary thing going, they're real documentary freaks, and they got a documentary about a circus fire, some old circus fire. And invited me over...

COREY: We could always um, we could always just get together later on, join up and...you know, just read in bed or something. That used to be fun.

ALEX: Oh, you always liked to do that, which is, really, to be honest, I found that incredibly boring and stupid. I mean that was one of those "Oh we've only been dating a few months so I'll go along with this because he seems to like it" kind of thing. I mean, it's Saturday night you know. We can read in bed any night, it's stupid to do it on our one real night of the week to go *out. (Pause.)*

COREY: I didn't know you didn't like that.

ALEX: I thought it was your polite way of saying you wanted to have sex, honestly. I thought you were maybe just shy about it and wanted an excuse to get into bed. Which would be *really* stupid.

COREY: You know me. Speaking of, like, things then and things *now* you know, I was just realizing that when we started dating you never said— you were not so—*opinionated.* Using these—horrible words. "Stupid." "Dumb." And I am. Really. I am sick of these. Judgments. All the time, all these *opinions*—

ALEX: Oh wait a second—

COREY: No, no, now wait, no, everything's, everything's either *this* or *that* or *good* or *bad* or *I like this rug it's classy* but *I hate that lamp it's you know* or *Oh that movie with that actor oh he is dreadful. (Pause.)*

ALEX: Well. I think it's pretty obvious that there's nothing either of us really wants to *do* tonight.

COREY: Well. Barbara and Ellen are really interesting. You're welcome to come.

ALEX: Michelle and Gregory are good people, you know, I don't know why you're always so—I mean, they watch documentaries, you know? They're not out boozing it up and being self-loathing about their appearances.

COREY: Well, Barbara and Ellen don't sit at home and watch a documentary and after that's over put some wine and cheese on the futon and sit around judging the moralities of those who have actually had some experience of *success* in their lives.

ALEX: Okay, Barbara and Ellen? Number one, they're grown women who have no love in their lives okay? They are cynical and they are dangerous and they are looking to wreck any lives they can, including their own, because they have *no idea what to do with their time.* So, so, if you ask me, there's a much greater joy to be had in watching a documentary and being one of the few people left on this planet who accepts the notion of history— remember that, we actually studied that in college, remember? —and does something about trying to keep it alive, instead of ordering feminine drinks with vulgar names and discussing each new ephemeral fad you've read about in *Vanity Fair.*

COREY: Well, that's a pretty revealing opinion. Calling Showcase Cinemas, we've got that projectionist you've been looking for!

ALEX: At least *I* know how to *mourn.*

COREY: Excuse me? Did I miss a line?

ALEX: People, people like Barbara and Ellen, they're ignorant. Okay, they would never *think* to watch a documentary, and, and mourn the sad, the terrible things that have happened in history, to, to people who are *not them.* All they mourn are the sad things that have happened to their *private parts.* There *are* greater things in this world than, than little stories of sex and business deals and *cocktails* and *home decorating!*

COREY: Yeah, apparently self-loathing, intellectual elitism is at the top of the list! *(Pause.)*

ALEX: All right now. We're past the five-minute mark, this is officially a fight.

COREY: Yeah well. It sounds like it could go on forever so. Maybe we should stop here.

ALEX: These are pretty severe ideological differences.

COREY: Well, these are questions of joy—others' joy, and our own.

ALEX: Well…joy, yes. But also…predictability, stagnation, the limitations of experience and communion, upper-middle-class young urban professional social rituals, fear of originality, the blatant *banality* and *cynicism* of the entertainment industry…

(Pause. Both look at each other.)

COREY: Well. Maybe we should just. Put on some music. And. Maybe we could both take baths.

ALEX: That might be nice.

COREY: Relaxing.

ALEX: Low key.

COREY: *(About to get up, stops.)* Oh, there's that play?...

ALEX: Play?...

COREY: Yeah, remember, that play that's playing over...

(Alex stares at Corey.)

COREY: *(Shaking his head.)* Yeah, you're right, I don't know what I'm thinking. So. Why don't you start the bath. And I'll run out and buy us some ice cream.

ALEX: Good. *(Corey rises.)*

COREY: See, this is. Here we are in agreement. I mean clearly we understand the simple pleasures.

ALEX: The joy of simplicity.

COREY: You know, sometimes I wish I'd been a Shaker.

ALEX: Sometimes I wish we didn't have all this money.

COREY: We didn't have it when we met, remember?

ALEX: I remember.

COREY: So many choices.

ALEX: So many *people*. I remember when it was just us. Alone on a Saturday night.

COREY: We didn't do *anything* really. *(Pause. Corey gets up.)* Cookie Dough okay?

ALEX: Cookie Dough okay. *(Corey gives a smile and a wave and goes. Alex sighs, looks around. Stands. Smile dies. Sits. Looks at her watch.)* Six-forty. *(Blackout.)*

END OF PLAY

Joan of Arkansas
by Sheri Wilner

CHARACTERS

LAURA: twenty-six to twenty-nine, a college student.

DENNIS: nineteen to twenty-one, a college student.

SETTING

A reading room in the library of a large university. Present day.

PLAYWRIGHT'S NOTE ON THE SCRIPT

Throughout the script there are moments in which the audience must realize that time is passing; however, this should not be achieved through the use of blackouts, which should not occur at any point in the play.

Joan of Arkansas

A reading room in a college library. Academic and elegant.

Laura is sitting at a long, wooden table with books and papers piled around her. On the table there are small, antique desk lamps spaced evenly apart.

Dennis enters carrying a large backpack which he places on a chair at the other end of the table. He removes a book from his backpack and sets it on the table. He proceeds to take out about fifteen books, one by one. The effect should be similar to that of clowns piling out of a tiny car at the circus. He then organizes the books in some specific order. When all his books are out, he sits down and begins to work. They both write silently. After a beat, they look at each other.

DENNIS: Finals week. Fun time.

LAURA: Yeah.

DENNIS: I thought I was the only one stuck with a final on the last day.

LAURA: You're not.

(Sound: clock ticking. Ticking stops. It is half an hour later. They are absorbed in their papers. All of a sudden, a strange noise is heard. It is the flurry of wings. Laura looks up at a bookshelf and sees a small bird perched on top. She is shocked to see a bird in a library. She looks at Dennis who has noticed it too. They smile and resume their work.)

(Sound: clock ticking. Ticking stops. It is half an hour later. Laura and Dennis are sitting in contorted positions, trying to see the bird underneath the table. Dennis places his cupped hand on the floor. Laura resumes her work.)

DENNIS: Excuse me?

LAURA: Yes?

DENNIS: Could you just...push it a little? Toward my hand.

LAURA: I'm afraid I'll scare it.

DENNIS: You won't. Just lead it toward me.

(Laura gently extends her hand. They remain in their positions for several seconds before he finally gives up. He and Laura politely smile.)

(Sound: clock ticking. Ticking stops. It is half an hour later. Laura and Dennis are looking more tired and stressed. Sounds of the bird can still be heard. They occasionally look up at the bird, now with slight impatience. Laura looks over her shoulder.)

LAURA: Every desk is free. I should move.

DENNIS: I've written my last three papers at this desk. This is due tomorrow, I can't take any chances... Does that sound crazy? *(Laura holds up her pen and shows it to Dennis.)*

LAURA: Without this, I'm nothing.

(Sound: clock ticking. Ticking stops. It is half an hour later. It is slightly darker in the room. Laura turns on a desk lamp and looks pleased at the light it casts on the desk. She moves over one seat so that her papers are directly under the light. Dennis has seen this.)

DENNIS: First time here?

LAURA: How'd you know? *(The bird flies by; they watch it.)*

DENNIS: Lucky guess. *(Dennis turns on the desk lamp nearest him.)* It's the chairs that keep me coming back. Makes me feel like I'm in the Oval Office. *(Laura smiles and nods politely.)* So...you think you'll come here again? Now that you've discovered this oasis?

LAURA: Yeah. Probably. I probably will.

(They smile at each other. The bird flies by. Beat.)

(Sound: clock ticking. Ticking stops. It is half an hour later. Laura is holding a bagel in her hands. She rips tiny pieces from it and places the crumbs in a row in front of her. Once she has placed a substantial amount of crumbs down, she sits. They wait for the bird to land in front of them. It doesn't. After a moment, they look at each other, embarrassed. The bird lands on the table. Laura gasps. As she studies the bird Dennis watches her. Laura slowly extends her cupped hand towards the bird, hoping to catch it. It flies away.)

DENNIS: *(Smitten and entranced.)* What's your major?

LAURA: English. You?

DENNIS: History. *(Beat.)* Nice to meet you, English.

LAURA: Nice to meet you too, History. *(Beat.)* Laura.

DENNIS: Dennis.

LAURA: *(Pointing to her paper.)* Oscar Wilde.

DENNIS: *(Pointing to his paper.)* Joan of Arc.

(Laura smiles broadly. Beat.)

*(Sound: clock ticking. Ticking stops. It is half an hour later. The bird is fly-
ing around. Laura and Dennis look more tired and haggard. Dennis crum-
ples a piece of paper with annoyance.)*

DENNIS: This is stupid. I'm moving. *(He starts stuffing books into his bag. He
also makes a small stack, which he places under his arm.)* Good luck with
Oscar.

LAURA: Good luck with Joan. *(Dennis exits. Laura watches the bird fly around,
then walks to the windows and attempts to open them. They are bolted shut.
She locates the lock but can't figure out how to unlock it. She moves on to the
next window. No success there either. She looks up at the bird, which sits on a
perch by the window.)* Doesn't make sense does it? It's just one thin piece
of glass that's keeping you out of the sky. *(Laura stares at the sky through
the window. After a few seconds Dennis enters with all his books.)*

DENNIS: No use. I can't write anywhere else. *(Laura faces Dennis. He begins
unpacking his books.)*

*(Sound: clock ticking. Ticking stops. It is half an hour later. Dennis is stand-
ing next to the table. He is holding a wastebasket upside down and is poised
to bring it down on the bird, which has landed on the floor.)*

LAURA: That's a good idea.

*(Dennis approaches the bird, very slowly, when he gets near it, he quickly sets
the wastebasket down. Dennis and Laura watch the bird fly away.)*

LAURA: Well, in theory it was a good idea.

DENNIS: *(Holds up wastebasket.)* It's exactly how they caught Joan.

LAURA: *(Playing along.)* Really?

DENNIS: Yep. She was in a field somewhere listening to her voices when some
English soldiers came up behind her with a huge wastebasket and then...
Whomp.

LAURA: How weird. They got Oscar Wilde that way too. He was sitting in
some fancy restaurant, eating chocolates and drinking champagne, when
all of a sudden... *Whomp,* he's doing time in Reading Gaol.

DENNIS: Eerie coincidence, isn't it?

LAURA: Sure is.

*(Desperate to sustain the conversation, Dennis scrambles though his papers
then holds up a picture.)*

DENNIS: This is where they kept her locked up for a year.

LAURA: In there?

DENNIS: Yeah. Can you believe it?

LAURA: *(Takes the picture and studies it.)* A year. And she was what? Eighteen?

DENNIS: Nineteen.

(The bird flies past, Laura watches it. Dennis takes the picture from her.)

DENNIS: Sorry. I didn't mean to depress you.

LAURA: I was already depressed. *(She selects a book, opens to a marked page, and reads:)* "Suffering is one long moment. We cannot divide it by seasons. We can only record its moods, and chronicle their return." He wrote that in prison.

DENNIS: "I would rather do penance by dying than bear any longer the agony of imprisonment." She said that in prison.

LAURA: *(Pointing to the bird.)* I think our friend here would agree with Joan.

DENNIS: *(Impulsively.)* Would you?

LAURA: Would I—?

DENNIS: Rather die than be in prison? *(Beat.)* Don't answer. That was a stupid question. I don't—

LAURA: I'd rather die. Wouldn't you?

DENNIS: I—I don't know…I—

LAURA: Haven't you ever been somewhere and thought you'd never get out? And that the air around you was made of brick?

DENNIS: Are you a grad student?

LAURA: *(Shaking her head no.)* Senior. Why?

DENNIS: You seem…older.

LAURA: I am. I…waited awhile before starting school.

DENNIS: Oh yeah? What did you do? Travel?

LAURA: No. *(The bird flies by. Laura watches the bird.)*

DENNIS: That's what I should have done. The summer before coming here, me and some friends drove cross-country. Actually, cross-country isn't the right term. We sort of…did laps. Up and down, up and down, making our way west. We wanted to go to every state.

LAURA: Did you?

DENNIS: We missed some. I should have kept going. I don't know why but…but I'd like to say I've been to every state.

LAURA: Maybe this summer you can.

DENNIS: Which state are you from?

LAURA: One that I'm sure you missed.

DENNIS: I've been to both Dakotas.

LAURA: Arkansas.

DENNIS: You're from Arkansas? People really come from Arkansas?

LAURA: Yes. They do.

DENNIS: Let me guess. You come from "a town called Hope."

LAURA: If they had called my town Hope, I would have made them rename it. *(Laura watches the bird fly by.)* How do you think it got in here?

DENNIS: I'm not even sure how I got in here. *(Laura smiles. Dennis continues, no longer subtle.)* But I'm glad I did. *(They look at each other and notice the mutual attraction. The bird lands near them. Dennis retrieves the wastebasket, slowly stalks the bird, and then suddenly brings the basket down over it.)* Got it! Here hold it down.

LAURA: *(Talking to the bird in the wastebasket.)* Sshh. This will all be over soon. Very, very soon— *(Dennis has retrieved a large stack of books. He puts them on top of the wastebasket.)*

LAURA: What are you doing?

DENNIS: We finally caught it. I'm not taking any chances—

LAURA: You're— You're not going to bring it outside?

DENNIS: Outside? I didn't really think about it.

LAURA: But—

DENNIS: What?

LAURA: You're writing about Joan of Arc.

DENNIS: Not very well. Not with a bird flying all over the place.

LAURA: Can you take your books off? Please.

DENNIS: You saw how hard it was to catch. If we let it out again—

LAURA: You can't leave it in there.

DENNIS: Look, I have too much work to do. I haven't been able to do anything since I sat down.

LAURA: Well maybe if you stopped talking to me—

DENNIS: Hey, you could have said—

LAURA: I want to let it outside.

DENNIS: The second you tip this over, it'll fly away.

LAURA: I'll be careful.

DENNIS: There's air in here—

LAURA: It's hitting against the— Can't you hear it?

DENNIS: I have to write this paper.

LAURA: Move your books.

DENNIS: Calm down.

LAURA: MOVE YOUR BOOKS!!

DENNIS: NO!

(Laura grabs a desk lamp and smashes it against the window. The window breaks.)

DENNIS: Holy shit! *(Dennis moves away from the wastebasket. Laura turns it over, scoops the bird into her hands and releases it outside.)*

LAURA: It was trapped.

DENNIS: Yeah, but you—

LAURA: It was trapped.

DENNIS: Shit. A guard's coming. *(Dennis hastily gathers up his books and exits. From offstage, he speaks to a guard.)* No, not me. I had nothing to do with it.

(Laura walks to the window and looks outside.)

END OF PLAY

A Play for
Two Actors, Either Gender

Tape
by José Rivera

CHARACTERS

PERSON

ATTENDANT

Tape

A small dark room. No windows. One door. A Person is being led in by an Attendant. In the room is a simple wooden table and chair. On the table is a large reel-to-reel tape recorder, a glass of water, and a pitcher of water.

PERSON: Dark in here.

ATTENDANT: I'm sorry.

PERSON: No, I know it's not your fault.

ATTENDANT: I'm afraid of those lights…

PERSON: I guess, what does it matter now?

ATTENDANT: …not very bright.

PERSON: Who cares, really?

ATTENDANT: We don't want to cause you an undue suffering. If it's too dark in here, I'll make sure one of the other attendants replaces the light bulb.
(The Person looks at the Attendant.)

PERSON: Any "undue suffering?"

ATTENDANT: That's right. *(The Person looks at the room.)*

PERSON: Is this where I'll be?

ATTENDANT: That's right.

PERSON: Will you be outside?

ATTENDANT: Yes.

PERSON: The entire time?

ATTENDANT: The entire time.

PERSON: Is it boring?

ATTENDANT: I'm sorry?

PERSON: Is it boring? You know. Waiting outside all the time.

ATTENDANT: *(Soft smile.)* It's my job. It's what I do.

PERSON: Of course. *(Beat.)* Will I get anything to eat or drink?

ATTENDANT: Well, we're not really set up for that. We don't have what you'd call a kitchen. But we can send out for things. Little things. Cold food.

PERSON: I understand.

ATTENDANT: Soft drinks.

PERSON: *(Hopefully.)* Beer?

ATTENDANT: I'm afraid not.

PERSON: Not even on special occasions like my birthdays?

ATTENDANT: *(Thinking.)* I guess maybe on your birthday.

PERSON: *(Truly appreciative.)* Great, thanks. *(Beat.)*

ATTENDANT: Do you have any more questions before we start? Because if you do, that's okay. It's okay to ask as many questions as you want. I'm sure you're very curious. I'm sure you'd like to know as much as possible, so you can figure out how it all fits together and what it all means. So please ask. That's why I'm here. Don't worry about the time. We have a lot of time. *(Beat.)*

PERSON: I don't have any questions.

ATTENDANT: *(Disappointed.)* Are you sure?

PERSON: There's not much I really have to know is there? Really?

ATTENDANT: No, I guess not. I just thought…

PERSON: It's okay. I appreciate it. I guess I really want to sit.

ATTENDANT: Sit. *(The person sits on the chair and faces the tape recorder.)*

PERSON: Okay, I'm sitting.

ATTENDANT: Is it…comfortable?

PERSON: Does it matter? Does it really fucking matter?

ATTENDANT: No. I suppose not. *(The Attendant looks sad. The Person looks at the Attendant and feels bad.)*

PERSON: Hey I'm sorry. I know it's not your fault. I know you didn't mean it. I'm sorry.

ATTENDANT: It's all right.

PERSON: What's your name anyway? Do you have a name?

ATTENDANT: Not really. It's not allowed.

PERSON: Really? Not allowed? Who says?

ATTENDANT: The rules say.

PERSON: Have you actually seen these rules? Are they in writing?

ATTENDANT: Oh yes. There's a long and extensive training course.

PERSON: *(Surprised.)* There is?

ATTENDANT: Oh yes. It's quite rigorous.

PERSON: Imagine that.

ATTENDANT: You have to be a little bit of everything. Confidant, confessor, friend, stern taskmaster. Guide.

PERSON: I guess that would take time.

ATTENDANT: My teachers were all quite strong and capable. They really pushed me. I was grateful. I knew I had been chosen for something unique and exciting. Something significant. Didn't mind the hard work and sleepless nights.

PERSON: *(Surprised.)* Oh? You sleep?

ATTENDANT: *(Smiles.)* When I can. *(Beat.)*

PERSON: Do you dream? *(Beat.)*

ATTENDANT: No. *(Beat.)* That's not allowed. *(Beat.)*

PERSON: I'm sorry.

ATTENDANT: No. It's something you get used to.

PERSON: *(Trying to be chummy.)* I know. I went years and years without being able to remember one single dream I had. It really scared the shit out of me when I was ten and…

ATTENDANT: I know.

PERSON: I'm sorry.

ATTENDANT: I said I know. I know that story. When you were ten.

PERSON: Oh. Yeah. I guess you would know everything. Every story.

ATTENDANT: *(Apologetic.)* It's part of the training.

PERSON: I figured. *(A long uncomfortable silence.)*

ATTENDANT: *(Softly.)* Have you ever operated a reel-to-reel tape recorder before?

PERSON: No I haven't. I mean—no.

ATTENDANT: It's not hard.

PERSON: I, uhm, these things were pretty obsolete by the time I was old enough to afford stereo equipment, you know, I got into cassettes, and, later, CDs, but never one of these jobbies.

ATTENDANT: It's not hard. *(Demonstrates.)* On here. Off here. Play. Pause. Rewind.

PERSON: *(Surprised.)* Rewind?

ATTENDANT: In some cases the quality of the recording is so poor…you'll want to rewind it until you understand.

PERSON: No fast forward?

ATTENDANT: No.

PERSON: It looks like a pretty good one. Sturdy. Very strong.

ATTENDANT: They get a lot of use.

PERSON: I bet. *(Beat.)* Is this the only tape? *(The Attendant laughs out loud— then quickly stops.)*

ATTENDANT: No.

PERSON: I didn't think so.

ATTENDANT: There are many more.

PERSON: How many? A lot?

ATTENDANT: There are ten thousand boxes.

PERSON: *Ten* thousand?

ATTENDANT: I'm afraid so.

PERSON: Did I really...

ATTENDANT: I'm afraid you did.

PERSON: So...everyone goes into a room like this?

ATTENDANT: Exactly like this. There's no differentiation. Everyone's equal.

PERSON: For once.

ATTENDANT: What isn't equal, of course, is the...amount of time you spend here listening.

PERSON: Oh God.

ATTENDANT: *(Part of the training.)* Listening, just to yourself. To your voice.

PERSON: I know.

ATTENDANT: Listening, word by word, to every lie you ever told while you were alive.

PERSON: Oh God!

ATTENDANT: Every ugly lie to every person, every single time, every betrayal, every lying thought, every time you lied to yourself, deep in your mind, we were listening, we were recording, and it's all in these tapes, ten thousand boxes of them, in your own words, one lie after the next, over and over, until we're finished. So the amount of time varies. The amount of time you spend here all depends on how many lies you told. How many boxes of tape we have to get through together.

PERSON: *(Almost in tears.)* I'm sorry...

ATTENDANT: Too late.

PERSON: I said I'm sorry! I said I'm sorry! I said it a million times! What happened to forgiveness? I don't want to be here! I don't want this! I don't want to listen! I don't want to hear myself! I didn't mean to say the things that I said! I don't want to listen!

ATTENDANT: Yes, well. Neither did we. Neither did we. *(The Attendant looks sadly at the Person. The Attendant turns on the tape recorder. The Attendant hits the Play button, the reels spin slowly, and the tape starts snaking its way through the machine. Silence. The Attendant leaves the room, leaving the Person all alone. The Person nervously pours a glass of water, accidentally spilling water on the floor. From the depths of the machine comes a long-forgotten voice.)*

WOMAN'S VOICE: "Where have you been? Do you know I've been looking all over? Jesus Christ! I went to Manny's! I went to the pharmacy! The school! I even called the police! Look at me, Jesus Christ, I'm shaking! Now look at me—look at me and tell me where the hell you were! Tell me right now!" *(Silence. As the Person waits for the lying response, the lights fade to black.)*

END OF PLAY